D0977318

Someone's
in the
Kitchen
with Dinah

Someone's in the Kitchen with Dinah

Dinah Shore

Doubleday and Company, Inc./Garden City, New York

Publishing Consultant: J. P. TARCHER, INC.

Copyright © 1971 by Dinah Shore

Library of Congress Catalog Card Number 77-154681

Designed by Miller/A. Schleifer

Manufactured in the United States of America

SECOND PRINTING, 1971

Introduction

❧

I have been collecting and trying recipes ever since I can remember.
I try to recreate them from having watched someone prepare a dish
or from simply having tasted it. I'm one of the original dyed-in-the-
wool "You order some of that and I'll order some of this and we'll
split" and "This is marvelous! How's yours? Well, maybe just a taste"
new-dish addicts, food touts, "just one more" incurables. I'll cook
for two or twenty or anything in between—which is the reason you'll
find so many open-end dinners here, meals that can be stretched for
drop-ins, shrunk for drop-outs and saved for another occasion.

The Someone in the Kitchen with Dinah is generally Pauline
Bumann, who's been with me twenty years and who is the living
refutation of the myth that a great cook has to be a plump one. Pauline is a lean, great cook—maybe because she runs, not walks to the
nearest pot simmering on some burner. We both love to entertain
and to mix our guests and our dishes.

I have included recipes which are old favorites that feature a
return to the basics—the chicken fricassee and dumplings or chicken
on corn bread, braised lamb shanks with white beans, pot roast with
kasha, stuffed pork chops or even soul food. These dishes invariably
turn out to be the favorites of my most traveled friends who constantly dine in the "best" restaurants in Paris, London, New York or
Rome. On the other hand, for friends from back home, who indulge
in these homey basics daily, I have also included the dishes I serve
to them, such as delicately sauced Seafood Crêpes, thinnest Veal with
Water Chestnuts or Veal Piccata, Potage Senegalese, Crown Roast of
Lamb with a barley casserole or pilaff.

I have included fat recipes—heavy, marvelous don't-give-a-damn
gorgeous gorgers, and if you look closely and study the fine print,
you'll find buried in here an occasional diet recipe. I had a much
larger number which lost out in the interests of editing to the fat-fun
ones. Some of the diet ones are sneaky because they allow you to
diet without being obvious and admitting you're a mere mortal and
have to watch it like everybody else. These are great ones for your

husband, boy friend, kids. (No, I take that back—most kids are impossible. It's the same dull thing time after time—fried chicken, hamburgers, french fries, potato chips, tacos, pizza, etc., but if they have a weight problem, they generally appreciate well seasoned, nicely served dinners with a little family conviviality thrown in with the parsley.)

I'm not a great one for cocktail parties, but there is something lovely about a small gathering at the cocktail hour, and I must say we do have a stream of drop-ins around that time at Dinah's Bar & Grill. The cocktail hour is generally the time when people are more relaxed or hungrier and more likely to try something new. For that reason, you will find a great number of hors d'oeuvres or "openers." It's a great way to empty the freezer, use leftovers or experiment with a new dish on a smaller scale before you try it for a whole meal.

You'll find a Ratatouille that cleans out the vegetable bin and cooler and the many variations of hot soups, cold soups, salads, vegetables that do the same. You'll find one-dish meals, such as Cioppino, Chicken Soup-Stew, Moussaka, Corned Beef and Cabbage, Beef-Chicken Tamale Pie, which you can really handle and still be with your company and not in the kitchen the whole time. You'll find homemade ice creams (are there any other kind?) guaranteed dietetic and otherwise, cookies, open fruit pies, closed fruit pies, pound cakes, fudge cakes, rum cakes, apple pots, tarts, tortes, chocolate soufflés, pots au crème. All these beautiful, soon to be abandoned forever ultimates in a fine meal because nobody wants to be fat anymore, are lovingly presented here not only because they are such fun to make and serve, but because they are the show stoppers that let you know you've done it again!

A word of thanks to my dear tennis "bums." They'll eat almost anything and most of my testing was done on them. Cooking is one thing, but cooking a dish the same way twice, measuring it exactly and writing it down is quite another. I forced myself to place a measuring cup under "a handful of this" or a spoon under each "pinch of that" and tried not to be self-consciously different about the feel of the dish in the process. Many's the Saturday or Sunday afternoon after tennis buffets of three or four main dishes—light little snacks like Creole Jambalaya and Cassoulet and Tennessee Lasagna, a couple of salads, four or five carefully tested, approved or rejected desserts— we'd waddle out to the court to try to play it off, not wiser but a little slower perhaps and surely less competitive. I think among us we gained 100 pounds while this cookbook was being written. They're desperately trying to get back into shape for their tournaments before I start the sequel.

I haven't gone too far into a most important food factor and that is the way it is presented and served, the way the flowers or center-piece of any kind, such as fruit, vegetables, vines, branches, etc. are arranged, the way the buffet table is set up and the platter decorated. These don't have to be costly or time-consuming efforts. It just takes a little prodding of your own imagination to use everything you have around the house in varied ways instead of running out to buy what was pictured in last week's Sunday supplement.

I have occasionally suggested the rest of the menu with the entrée so that you won't make the mistake I've made from time to time of not balancing a heavy meal with a light salad and dessert or of having a richly sauced dish for your main course as well as the first one. That gooey dessert could be a triumph after a simple broiled salmon or beef dinner and a disaster after a pork roast with sauerkraut and apples.

I've written a little note preceding some of the recipes. Please don't feel for a moment that the unanecdoted ones are less precious to me than the ones I've urged you to try for some reason or other. As a matter of fact, the anecdoted ones are like misunderstood children—I feared you might not see their beauty without a little explana-tion as to where, how and how come.

It should be obvious that I love to cook and entertain and do it often and informally in a variety of ways because I got bored with the perfectly broiled eye of beef, string beans and puréed peas in arti-choke bottoms that seem to grace so many dinner parties where money was no object and effort and imagination the same.

I never got a standing ovation for a pot roast—but it feels like it when they go back for seconds.

Dinah Shore

Beverly Hills, March 1971

P.S. From time to time in this book you will see various goodies with the possessive Bea's, such as Bea's Brownies, Bea's Wilted Spinach Salad. Bea is Bernice Korshak, a dear friend of long standing. We have played, shopped, cried or laughed together through many vicissitudes in both our lives. One constant was our love of good foods (once we even traveled through Europe—not by road map—but by the stomach, literally deciding where we wanted to go and when, according to what restaurant we'd heard about).

Often, when our children were smaller, we'd play six to eight sets of tennis, race to Farmer's Market in our tennis clothes, buy everything we needed, race home and start cooking a gourmet dinner still in our tennis shorts under disapproving, impatient glances from our spouses and collected kids. In record time we threw together incredible, lavish and, if I must admit it, delicious meals. They always forgave us. What could they do? They knew we were going to go right back to the same routine the next day. Nobody ever missed a meal and we didn't get fat. (Now that I think of it, we could have played four sets of tennis and had more time and less grousing.) I will admit we did a little preparation before we tore off in the mornings for our first match.

Bea, who is indefatigable, along with my sister, Bessie, and other close sympathetic friends we could draft into the kitchen, helped Pauline and me test and retest many of the dishes I hope you will be enjoying from this book.

Contents

❧

Tips for Party Planning 15

Eggs, Brunch and Breads

Sunday Baked Eggs 20
Omelette Grand Mère 21
Sunday Steak and Biscuits 22
Biscuits 23
Eggs à la Basque 24
Jody's Eggs 24
Kathie Browne McGavin's Huevos Rancheros 25
French Toast 26
Corned Beef Hash 27
Cousin Selma's Pancake 28
Cornmeal Pancakes 28
Creole Corn Muffins 29
Popovers 30
Gougère 31
Hot Water Hoecake 32

For Openers

Chicken Wings 34
Chicken or Turkey Water Chestnut Balls 35
Quesadillas 36
Mushrooms and Sour Cream 36
Mushrooms and Sweet Cream 37
Pauline's Baked Mushrooms 38
Japanese Shrimp 38
Florentine Grilled Shrimp 39
Shrimp Balls 40
Shrimp Arnaud 41
Shrimp and Crab Buccaneer 41
Chopped Chicken Liver 42
Big Deal Chopped Chicken Liver or Chicken Liver Paté 43
Sicilian Eggplant Caponata 44

Herring Salad 44

Steak Tartare 45

Steak or Chicken Teriyaki 46

Pauline's Deviled Egg Salad 47

Buttered Tiny Thin Biscuits with Country Fried Ham 48

Soups

Pauline's Onion Soup 50

Fresh Pea Soup 50

Pumpkin Soup 51

Spinach Soup.. 52

Navy Bean Soup 53

Quick Purée Mongol 53

Minestrone 54

Mother's Borscht 54

Gazpacho 55

Potage Senegalese (Iced Chicken and Curry Soup) 56

Cold Cucumber Soup 56

The Main Dish

MEATS

Beef Stroganoff and Kasha.............................. 58

Brisket of Beef with Puréed Vegetable Gravy 59

Pauline's Corned Beef and Cabbage; Mustard Sauces 60

Bill Holden's Marinated Hawaiian Steak 61

Meat Loaf 62

Hamburgers with Almonds 63

Filled Hamburgers 64

Pepper Hamburger Steak 64

Hamburger De Luxe 65

Calves' Liver Veneziana................................ 65

Brown Stock and Brown Sauce (Sauce Espagnole) 66

Veal Chasseur 67

Veal Piccata 68

Veal Scaloppine with Cheese 68

Veal Birds with Pine Nuts 69

Veal Birds with Water Chestnuts 70

Crown Roast of Lamb with Barley Pilaff 71

Rack of Lamb 72

Lamb Shanks with White Beans 72

Indonesian Satay — A Shish Kebab 74
Lamb Shish Kebab 74
Baked Stuffed Pork Chops; Fresh Applesauce 75
Barbecued Spareribs 76
Barbecued Ham or Pork 77
Barbecue Sauce 77
Audrey Wilder's Smoked Pork Loin and Sauerkraut 78
Sausage and Peppers 79

FISH AND SHELLFISH

Cioppino 80
Red Snapper 82
Crab Cakes 82
Stuffed Deviled Crab in Shells 83
Creole Jambalaya 84
Shrimps de Jonghe 84
Goujonnettes of Sole with Tartar Sauce 85
Pauline's Seafood Crêpes 86
Shrimp Creole 87

POULTRY—CHICKEN, DUCK AND TURKEY

Deviled Broiled Chicken 88
Broilers Hungarian................................. 88
Dr. Krohn's Mother's Chicken 89
Kleeman's Chicken on Corn Bread 90
Fried Chicken 91
Baked Fried Chicken 92
Fried Chicken Curry 92
Easy Roast Chicken and Almonds 93
Chicken Fricassee and Dumplings 94
Baking Powder Dumplings 94
Chicken in Parmesan Cream Sauce 94
The Benny's Roast Chicken 95
Different Chicken Soup-Stew (A Whole Meal) 96
Brown Chicken Pot Pie.............................. 96
Bea's Quick Top Crust 98
Chicken Marengo 98
Le Bistro Roast Duckling; Orange Sauce 99
Stuffing for Turkey or Chicken 101
Corn Bread 102

Day Later Turkey 102
Turkey Mornay 103

CASSEROLES AND ONE-DISH MEALS

Beef-Chicken Tamale Pie 104
Stuffed Cabbage 105
Cassoulet 106
Chicken Tetrazzini 107
Mother's Chili Con Carne 108
Baked Stuffed Eggplant 109
Moussaka 110
Black-Eyed Peas 111
Piroshki 112
Harmony McCoy's Soul Food 113
Tennessee Lasagna 114
Pastel de Choclo y Maiz (Chilean Meat and Corn Casserole) ..115
Sausage Cornmeal Pie 117

CHEESE, RICE, PASTA AND POTATOES

Cheese Pit 118
Le Bistro's Cheese Soufflé 118
Pauline's Cheese Soufflé 119
Macaroni and Red Wine Meat Sauce 120
Pasta Fazool 120
Parmesan Toast 121
Frank's Fresh Tomato Sauce for Spaghetti 122
Godfrey Cambridge's Spaghetti Alla Carbonara 122
Spaghettini with Prosciutto and Mushrooms 123
Spaghetti Sauce 124
Barley à La Tomato à La Colony Restaurant;
    Meat Sauce; Brown Sauce 124
Baked Hominy Grits with Cheese 126
Baked Pork and Beans 126
Red Beans and Rice 127
Potatoes à La Stockholm...............................128
Crusty Sweet Potato Puffs 129
Cheese Stuffed Baked Potatoes 129
Deep Fried Rice and Cheese Balls 130

VEGETABLES

String Beans Greek Style 131
Vegetable Gumbo Creole 132

Ratatouille 132
Vegetable Pie 133
Artichoke Hearts with Hollandaise Sauce; Hollandaise Sauce ..134
Asparagus Polonaise; Polonaise Sauce 135
Cauliflower with Cheese Sauce 136
Cabbage and Pine Nuts 136
Carrot Purée 137
Corn in Lettuce Leaf 138
Celery-Carrot Sauté 138

SALADS AND SALAD DRESSINGS

Vegetable Salad 140
Italian Salad..141
More Than Potato Salad 142
Salad Niçoise 142
Mother's Chicken Salad 143
Curried Chicken Salad 144
Bessie's and Mr. Hansen's Danish Cucumbers 144
Cucumbers in Dilled Sour Cream 145
Finger Salad 145
Louise's Marinated String Beans 146
Bea's Wilted Spinach Salad 146
Sour Cream Cheese Fruit Salad Mold 146
Pauline's French Dressing 148
Basic French Dressing 148
Vinaigrette Dressing 149
Jody's Favorite Russian Dressing 150

For Closers

DESSERTS AND PIES

Apple Pot 152
Apple Pancake 152
Kleeman's Apple Pie 154
Edana Romney's Fresh Plum Tart 154
Fresh Peach Pie 155
Orange Pie Filling 156
Pecan Crunch Pie 157
Fudge Pie 157
Crême Brulée 158
Cottage Cheese and Blueberry Pancakes 158

Gingerbread with Caramel Sauce 159
Pots au Crême 160
Prune Whip with Port Wine 160
Bea's Brownies 161
Maple Walnut Ice Cream 162
Pauline's Coffee Ice Cream 163
Unfattening Strawberry Ice Cream 163
English Rolled Wafers with Chocolate Fudge Sauce;
    Chocolate Fudge Sauce. 164
Rice Pudding from the Riviera Hotel .165
Very Chocolate-y Soufflé 166
Barley Soufflé 167

CAKES AND COOKIES

Mother's Pecan Rum Cakes 169
The Losers' Coffee Cake 170
Cinnamon Pound Cake 171
Coconut Pound Cake 172
Pauline's German Sweet Chocolate Cake 172
Fanny Brice's Super Chocolate Cake .173
Chocolate Date Cake with Whipped Cream Topping 174
Pecan Nut Balls. 175
Cheesecake Cookies 175
Quality Coconut Cookies in Quantity 176
Toffee Coffee Ice Cream Cake 177
Fruit Cake 178

Tips for Party Planning

As I said earlier, I love to entertain—and since I entertain often, I've developed a few principles on party giving which work well for me. I herewith present some of them for your consideration. I hope they'll be helpful.

If you have a large number of people to whom you're beholden or with whom you want to be, give two or three parties in a row. The flowers will still be fresh, leftovers may be surreptitiously used and—you won't have crowded thirty people together when you really could have handled fourteen more comfortably.

Be sure to tell your guests ahead of time how you plan to dress. There are few things more disconcerting than walking into a dinner dressed to the nines when everybody else is in slacks or vice versa. I like informal, comfortable attire. Black tie is for state occasions or the Grand Ballroom at the Biltmore. Maybe it's my California conditioning, but I always feel people have a better time when they're comfortable. Sometimes it's a little hard for New Yorkers to believe I'm sincere about the sport jacket and no tie, but once they get the hang of it, they're the first ones to take off their shoes too.

A sit-down place-carded party doesn't mean a formal one and I don't usually seat husbands and wives together. This simply means that on that drive home after the party when one mate inevitably says to his or her spouse, "How come you didn't sit with me at dinner?"— you are the guilty one. No matter how loving or adoring they are, husbands and wives drive to and from the party together, dress for it and undress from it in the same house, so they should get a chance to mingle with other guests without worrying about neglecting each other. The hostess should see that the shyer mate is surrounded, at least at dinner, with livelier extroverts. I feel even an informal buffet should have place cards.

You don't always have to seat people in the same old traditional way—boy, girl, boy, girl, etc. I happen to have a long dining table, not a round one, so I have on occasion seated ladies on one side—gents on the other. That way they can look at each other and chat more easily. Most women I know would rather look at a man any time.

I try to balance the guest list as well as the menu—same number of men as women, unattached or otherwise, but sometimes it doesn't come out that way and when it doesn't I try to remember a wonderful line by a writer named Harry Kurnitz, who said when seated next to a gentleman instead of a lady, "It's all right, we're here for dining, not mating."

If your party is over fifteen or twenty people and everyone can't sit at one table, set up individual tables for six or eight with a little decoration, silverware, glasses, napkins, salt and pepper. This will keep some helpless joker from balancing his filled plate, wine glass, knife, fork and napkin while looking around desperately for a place to put them besides his knees. It's a darned sight safer for your carpet and sofa too. Incidentally, I found large round covers that clamp on the top of my card tables at a local department store. They are lightweight, not too expensive, and they fold up for storage in the back of a closet. You can seat six nicely at these tables, and eight if you squeeze a little.

I don't like a too long pre-party drinking time. I think you really have to set a time for dining and stick to it. If somebody is terribly late and you have no way of knowing why, you worry a little, call to check and then go ahead and serve. There is no point in spoiling the meal for everyone else. The timing on your main dish may be important. One evening I invited a group of twelve for dinner. My guest of honor was a television star and his wife, both known for promptness. The guests were invited for 7:30. 7:30—8:30—9:00 came and went and at 9:30 we had dinner. To this day they haven't arrived. I took the place cards off last Wednesday—that's really late!

I may be a food tout, but I'm not a drink pusher. Some people simply don't like the stuff or maybe can't handle it. I have plenty of non-alcoholic choices around because really it's not the drink that counts in the cocktail hour—it's the company, the conversation, the ice tinkling in the glasses—the atmosphere. Incidentally, I always have enough ice around to service ten times the number I've invited. A large baggie or two of extra cubes in the freezer does the trick.

I always serve hors d'oeuvres with drinks—peanut and candy noshing is not conducive to the appreciation of that dinner you've worked so hard on.

Occasionally, a little menu card placed on the coffee table or in the bar is a good idea. Then if your guests like your proposed dinner menu, they won't fill up on hors d'oeuvres, and if they aren't too crazy about it, they can eat up and hold back later. (I have little porcelain menu stands and I write the menu on them with a felt pen. The ink can be washed off easily and the stands reused.) I say "occasionally" because I really like my dinner to be a surprise and I hope a delight.

One of the most useful things I have is my looseleaf party notebook with complete menus and guest lists, and if I can remember it, the seating arrangement. This saves me the embarrassment of serving the same people the same dish time and time again. I've been keeping this record for about fifteen years and I'm always amazed at how many menus and recipes and great groupings I'd forgotten about completely that come back fresh when I see them listed.

In my opinion, an adult party should be for adults and except for those family occasions when children and adults are invited together, children shouldn't be a lingering permanent fixture. They can nicely be made to feel part of the proceedings by greeting the guests, handling the wraps and perhaps passing the hors d'oeuvres, but it is kind of frustrating to be assigned someone's precocious eleven-year-old as a dinner partner who tries valiantly to be as entertaining as the grownups with his school and intramural sports for conversation material while you're getting a drift of a spicy interchange across the table about politics, women's lib, the Mideast situation or Masters and Johnson.

It is a nice idea, on the other hand, to throw a party for friends and their children and gear it to the mutual interests of both groups. In other words, don't seat the kids "over there," but keep everyone together. No fair correcting behavior and table manners. You'll be amazed at how they rise to the occasion and how stimulating the party and conversation can be.

A party with an idea behind it is easier, more fun to plan, and can bring that family feeling to a large gathering of strangers or relatives from all parts of the country who really have nothing in common but a twice-removed kissing cousin.

Once I gave a down home party. People wore overalls, tennis shoes, bluejeans, Mother Hubbards, etc. The buffet table was set up like the food contestant entrants I remembered from the Franklin County Fair in Tennessee. Each dish was labeled and had a blue or red ribbon attached—for instance, Mrs. Bumann's (Pauline's) 1st Prize Pecan Pie. Complete with red checkered tablecloths, watermelons and magnolia branches as centerpieces, candles in tin cups, jugs, fried chicken, biscuits and mashed potatoes and gravy, passed up and down the table and country music on the record player—it was fun!

Plan and prepare for your party well so you'll have time to enjoy it yourself. Do your menu, marketing and flower buying early in the morning or the day before, if possible. Have your flowers arranged, tables set, place cards made or have the seating arrangement in your head or hand beforehand. Try to plan dishes that can be done in advance so that you can be free to mingle and make everybody else comfortable too. Above all—be available when the guests arrive to make them welcome and, if necessary, to introduce them around.

If the soufflé fell and the casserole overflowed, chances are nobody will remember it, but they will remember if they were relaxed and had laughs. My daughter, Missy, and her group talk a lot about "good vibes." They mean vibrations from a room, a person or a gathering. We're all animals and we sense and respond to tension and calm in many ways. If the source—in this case, the hostess, is relaxed, confident and comfortable, her guests and atmosphere will reflect her and the party will give off "good vibes." Enjoy your party!

Eggs,
Brunch
and
Breads

Sunday brunch or Sunday morning breakfast is a big deal. It has to be to make up for all the grouchy weekdays when everybody is in a hurry and you've forced pancakes or eggs or hot cereal (in place of the cold packaged ones the kids want) and everybody goes his separate way full of food and hostility.

Sunday brunch usually takes place at a respectable hour so everybody can sleep late, including Mom, who still has time to read the paper and get a special breakfast together. This is one of them:

Sunday Baked Eggs

2 tomatoes sliced medium thick
8–10 eggs (figure on two
    per person)
6 slices of ham or Canadian bacon,
    thinly sliced and cut into
    wide strips

¼ cup bread crumbs
Salt and pepper to taste
Butter
½ cup grated American cheese
Cheese Sauce

Line buttered baking dish with ham or Canadian bacon. Lay tomato slices flat on ham. Salt and pepper generously. Break eggs over tomatoes carefully. Cover with Cheese Sauce. Top generously with grated American cheese, bread crumbs and butter dots. Bake in pre-heated 325° oven for 20 minutes (or longer if harder cooked eggs desired).

Cheese Sauce

½ cup of either Cheddar, Monterey
    Jack or Swiss Cheese (or
    combination of all), cubed
2 heaping tablespoons butter
2 tablespoons flour

1 cup plus 2 tablespoons milk
Dash of Worcestershire sauce
    (optional)
Dash of Tabasco sauce (optional)

Melt butter in pan and blend in flour; add milk very gradually, stirring constantly. When smooth and thickened, add bits of cheese, salt, pepper, dash each of Worcestershire and Tabasco.

Serves 4 or 5.

Omelette Grand Mère

I fell in love with this dish at the Four Seasons Restaurant in New York. Whenever I had a luncheon date, if anybody gave me the choice, I'd pick the Four Seasons—just so I could enjoy the Omelette Grand Mère again.

When the restaurant's manager—Stewart Levin—visited the West Coast one spring, he not only brought me the recipe and taught me to use it, but he brought me one of their heavy-duty omelette pans, too. I'd have married him on the spot, but his wife and kids objected.

◐

1 tablespoon melted butter
2 tablespoons bacon, fried crisp
   and crumbled
3 eggs
Pinch salt

Dash Tabasco sauce
1 teaspoon chives, chopped
1 teaspoon parsley, chopped
2 tablespoons Gruyère,
   freshly grated

Heat omelette pan. Add butter. While butter is melting, beat eggs with a wire whisk. Add salt, Tabasco, chives and parsley to the eggs. Pour the egg mixture into the hot butter and stir. Add bacon and continue stirring. When the omelette is just set (do not cook too long), sprinkle the cheese down the center of it, fold it and turn it out onto a warm plate. Serve at once. Be sure not to overcook. Do not fry the bacon in the omelette pan as it will ruin the omelette pan. In fact, don't fry anything in your omelette pan but your omelette. It's best not to double your recipe—have two omelette pans going if you have them—or you'll be cooking omelettes all day.

Serve this with buttered, toasted English muffins.

One serving.

Sunday Steak and Biscuits

4 sirloin steaks, cut very thin and then cut in half	Flour Salt and pepper to taste

Take half of Biscuit recipe (on the next page) and lift out to floured board. Pat dough gently until it is slightly thinner than usual. Cut biscuits with a large cutter (2—2½ inches in diameter) dipped in flour. Bake as indicated in recipe. Then trim off gristle and fat from steaks. Place meat between 2 pieces of wax paper and pound with flat side of mallet or cleaver to flatten a little.

Dip in flour seasoned with salt and pepper. Sauté quickly in hot butter in a large skillet, turning only once. Remove steaks to hot platter.

While you are doing this, the others can have orange juice, or grapefruit juice, or whatever juice is in season in the living room while dawdling over the Sunday paper, providing they come to breakfast the minute they are called. This dish can't wait any longer than a soufflé.

When biscuits are just done, place steak on bottom half of very hot biscuit. Pour a little gravy over it and cover with top half of biscuit. Serve immediately with scrambled eggs, crisp bacon, extra biscuits cut with your small regular cutter, extra gravy, extra butter and extra jam. Diet on Monday!

Serves 4 to 6.

Gravy

2 tablespoons seasoned flour used for steaks	Drippings left in pan 2 cups chicken broth, water or milk

Take the drippings left in the pan and add the seasoned flour you've used for the steaks. Stir flour into the drippings over a hot flame until brown. Add the chicken broth, water or milk, very gradually, stirring constantly. The gravy should not be too thick. Taste for seasoning. Let simmer until all flavors are blended.

If a less tender cut than sirloin is used, pound to break up tissues in meat and tenderize it. Pound in seasoned flour with a mallet or cleaver. When browned on both sides, remove to hot platter. After making gravy, return steaks to skillet and cook covered in gravy for 5 minutes or more or until they are tender.

Biscuits

2 cups sifted flour
2 teaspoons baking powder
½ teaspoon salt

½ cup shortening
1 cup + 2 tablespoons milk

Sift dry ingredients together into a medium-sized mixing bowl. Then add shortening. Cut shortening into flour mixture coarsely with 2 knives. Stir mixture gently while adding milk sparingly until dough is sticky and not dry. Lift dough out to a floured board, pat gently and cut with floured biscuit cutter. After the first batch is cut, pinch dough together, trying not to mix too much flour into it during the process.

Place on a greased cookie sheet so that biscuits don't touch. Put in a preheated 400° oven and bake for 10 minutes until nice and brown. You can brush the biscuits on the top with a little cream, which will give them a nice gloss.

Yields 16 small biscuits.

Eggs à la Basque

3 thin slices of ham, cut into strips	1 clove garlic, crushed
1 large tomato, sliced medium thick	Dash of cayenne
	Butter
1 medium onion, sliced medium thick	Cooking oil
	8 eggs
½ green pepper, cut into thin strips	½ cup milk
	Parsley, chopped

In oil to cover bottom of skillet, lightly sauté the slices of ham cut into strips. Remove from pan and keep warm. In same skillet, place a couple of teaspoons of butter, then add sliced onion and green pepper strips. Sauté gently until soft but not brown. Add salt and pepper and a dash of cayenne. Lay tomato slices over all; salt, cover, and cook over low flame 5 minutes or more. Remove cover; add crushed garlic. Raise the flame and cook quickly, shaking the skillet and turning it a little until most of the juice from the tomatoes cooks down. You can do this ahead of time.

In another heated skillet, place 2 tablespoons of butter. Beat eggs and add milk. Some people don't particularly like milk in their eggs — I'm one of them. A tablespoon of cream per egg is nice, but fattening. If you want to stretch this and feel virtuously thin, add an extra egg instead of cream, but the milk does seem to keep the eggs very light and fluffy. Season with salt and pepper. Pour the beaten eggs into the warm skillet and stir with a fork. When they begin to set, turn the heat down. Stir again. When just underdone, turn off the heat. It will continue cooking just from the heat of the pan. Let set while you assemble on heating serving dish. Place vegetables on the platter, and set eggs in the center. Garnish with reheated ham strips and parsley.

Serves 4.

Jody's Eggs

My son Jody makes the greatest scrambled eggs. I never could figure out why his were better than mine or Pauline's. Maybe it's because he's in a hurry.

He breaks his eggs in a bowl — beats them — seasons them and pours them into a hotter skillet than I would — with more butter than I would ordinarily use — swirls them around with the same fork he beat them with — and here's the trick — before they're what anybody else in the world would say cooked — he takes them off the heat. He checks his toaster, butters his toast — and then gives the eggs another swirl with the same fork out of the skillet on to his plate — light as air!

Some variations of Jody's Scrambled Eggs:

While he's cooking the eggs, I brown a hot dog (which I have cut into small cubes) in butter or margarine. Throw them in with the last swirl. Cubed bologna works and a salami pancake is great too! Simply fry thin slices of salami in a skillet on both sides in butter or margarine (2 pieces of salami and 3 eggs per customer). Add more butter. Pour beaten, slightly seasoned eggs over whole, lifting with fork to allow eggs to run over salami to bottom of pan for cooking. Flip over and out of pan and serve like a pancake.

Another variation:

Add 1 heaping tablespoon of cottage cheese per egg before scrambling, or 1 tablespoon grated Swiss cheese per egg before scrambling, or 1 heaping tablespoon sour cream per egg before scrambling.

Kathie Browne McGavin's Huevos Rancheros

Kathie and Darren McGavin were on my television show one of those mornings that started out like a warm puppy and moved on closer to a wet hen. Darren disagreed with a psychologist, who felt a lusty fight was good for the soul and the marriage. Darren couldn't even pretend to fight with Kathie. The psychologist requested a more volatile cast—maybe Burton and Taylor. I moderated. Kathie cooked these eggs and we ate them. The psychologist forgave us all—they were that good.

2 28-ounce cans tomatoes	2 teaspoons oregano
2 onions, finely chopped	Salt and pepper
¾ cup Jack or Muenster cheese	4 cloves garlic, finely chopped
and ¾ cup sharp Cheddar	2 dashes Tabasco sauce
cheese, mixed together	Olive oil
8 jalapenos (hot green chili	8 poached eggs
peppers), seeded	4 toasted tortillas

Sauté onions and garlic in a little olive oil until lightly browned. Add tomatoes, oregano and Tabasco sauce. Add jalapenos and salt and pepper. Taste for seasoning. Simmer until sauce is reduced by one-half.

Poach 8 eggs. Toast tortillas by holding over a gas flame with tongs, or by sautéing on both sides in a little oil in a skillet. Drain on paper towel. Keep warm until ready to assemble.

Remove jalapenos from sauce with slotted spoon and set aside. On each tortilla, place 2 poached eggs, pour sauce over eggs and place 2 jalapenos on top. Sprinkle cheese over top. Place under broiler just long enough to melt cheese.

Serves 4.

French Toast

I got this one from the Chef at the Racquet Club in Palm Springs many years ago. It is unusual and it is by far the best French toast I have ever tasted, especially when Pauline makes it. Definitely not for dieters.

6 slices of day-old egg bread sliced	1 egg
1 inch thick; cut crosswise	¼ teaspoon vanilla
1½ cups half and half	2 tablespoons powdered sugar

Beat half and half, egg, vanilla and one tablespoon powdered sugar together and strain through fine sieve into a bowl. Soak bread in liquid and place in pan containing 1 inch of butter. Cook slowly and turn often. Before serving sprinkle with remaining powdered sugar.

Some people insist on serving this with maple syrup, but this lily needs no gilding.

Serves 6.

Corned Beef Hash

I love to cook corned beef and cabbage—not only because it's delicious and almost impossible to louse up, but because I can make corned beef hash with the left overs. A dear man named Max Asnas, owner of the Stage Delicatessen on Broadway in New York (where else?) showed me how he makes it.

❧

2 cups cooked corned beef, cut into small chunks	2 tablespoons onions, grated
1 cup boiled potatoes, cubed	1 egg
	4 poached eggs

Pack beef, potatoes and onions together in a large mixing bowl. Place a plate on top and let it set overnight to meld and blend. The next morning add egg, lightly beaten, and mix thoroughly. Heat your griddle and add oil to the griddle. When the oil is very hot, place the corned beef hash, shaped into patties, on the griddle. Flatten with spatula as they cook. Cook until patties are crisp on both sides, turning carefully. Serve immediately with a poached egg on top.

Serve with hot, buttered rye or pumpernickel toast accompanied by whipped cream cheese and a little Bar-le-Duc or any tart jelly.

Serves 4.

Cousin Selma's Pancake

My cousin, Selma Lewis, was one of the most popular girls at Vanderbilt University when she was a student there. She's bright, pretty, laughs a lot and gloriously, and — something I didn't know until I visited her and her husband recently in Memphis — is also a great cook. Here's a sample:

❧

½ cup flour
½ cup milk
2 eggs, lightly beaten
Pinch of nutmeg

8 tablespoons butter
2 tablespoons sugar
Juice of half a lemon

Preheat oven to 325°. In a mixing bowl, combine the flour, milk, eggs, and nutmeg. Beat lightly, leaving batter a little lumpy. Melt butter in a 12-inch skillet with heatproof handle. When very hot, pour in batter. Bake in oven 15 to 20 minutes or until golden brown. Sprinkle with sugar and return briefly to oven. Sprinkle with lemon juice, then serve with jelly, jam, or marmalade.

Serves 4 to 6.

Cornmeal Pancakes

Pancakes are easy. Try these—they're deliciously different from everyday, ordinary buttermilk pancakes.

❧

1 cup yellow cornmeal
2 scant tablespoons sugar
1 teaspoon salt
1 cup boiling water
½ cup sifted all-purpose flour

2 teaspoons baking powder
1 egg
½ cup milk
2 tablespoons butter or
    margarine, melted

Combine cornmeal, sugar and salt in large bowl. Slowly stir in boiling water; cover, and let stand 10 minutes. Sift flour with baking powder; set aside. In a small bowl, beat egg, milk and butter until smooth. Pour into cornmeal batter, along with flour mixture, stirring quickly only until combined. Meanwhile, slowly heat griddle or heavy skillet. To test temperature, drop a little cold water onto hot griddle; water should roll off in drops. Use scant ¼ cup batter for each pancake. Cook until bubbles form on surface and edges become dry. Turn; cook 2 minutes longer, or until nicely browned on underside. Serve with melted butter and heated maple syrup.

Yields 10 four-inch cakes. Serves 4.

Creole Corn Muffins

1 cup yellow cornmeal	⅓ (generous) cup shortening
1 cup sifted flour	2 tablespoons green pepper,
2 teaspoons baking powder	finely chopped
Dash of cayenne	2 tablespoons onion, finely
1 teaspoon salt	chopped (optional)
1 cup milk	2 tablespoons pimento, chopped
1 egg	½ cup cheddar cheese, grated

Sift dry ingredients into a mixing bowl. Cut in the shortening until well blended. Add green pepper, onions, pimento and cheese. Add milk and eggs beaten together. Stir until just blended. (Don't worry about lumps.) Fill well-greased or teflon muffin tins two-thirds full. Bake in a preheated 400° oven about 15 minutes.

Yields 12 muffins.

Popovers

You may not be aware of it but there is a raging controversy about Popovers. It has to do with preheating or not preheating your oven and heating the Pyrex custard cups in which you bake them or not heating them. I heat and preheat! Craig Claiborne and Irma Rombauer, eat your heart out! That's the way "my momma done tol' me."

❧

1 cup flour, sifted	1 cup milk
½ teaspoon salt	1 tablespoon salad oil
2 eggs	

Preheat oven to 425°. Grease aluminum popover pans or large muffin tins (if you have an old iron popover pan all the better). I use Pyrex custard cups and grease them well and place on a baking sheet in the oven to heat thoroughly just before filling. Measure all ingredients into a bowl and beat with a rotary beater until mixture is very smooth. It is a thin batter, so don't worry about that. Fill cups a little less than half full and bake in the preheated oven about 30 minutes without peeking, or until the sides are rigid to the touch. If drier popovers are desired, pierce each one with a knife and bake five minutes longer.

The three tricks here are the preheated custard cups or muffin tins, filling them less than half full of batter so the popovers will have room to grow, and *not peeking*. I think it might work with door knobs if you follow these rules. Don't try it, however.

I use the Popovers instead of Yorkshire Pudding with roast beef.

Gougère

Gougère is a Swiss cheese quick bread. I admit I have led many people astray and off their diets with this irresistible hot bread accompanying an otherwise harmless, carefully calculated-down-to-the-last-calorie luncheon. But I always go with them, so the devil gets her just desserts —which I usually have the good grace to omit.

2 cups milk
½ cup butter
2 teaspoons salt
Dash of freshly ground black
    pepper
2 cups sifted flour

8 eggs
½ lb. natural Gruyère or
    Swiss cheese, cut into very
    fine cubes
Coarsely grated extra Gruyère
    or Swiss cheese

Scald the milk and cool it. Strain the milk into a large saucepan and add the butter, cut up, salt and pepper. Bring the mixture to a rolling boil and add all at once the sifted flour. Cook the paste over low heat, beating it briskly with a wooden spoon, until the mixture forms a ball and leaves the sides of the pan clean. Remove the pan from the heat and beat in the eggs, one at a time, incorporating each egg thoroughly before adding the next. When the paste is shiny and smooth mix in the cubed cheese. Let the dough cool.

Divide the dough in half. With an oval spoon scoop out from one half of the dough pieces the size of an egg. With a rubber spatula push them off the spoon onto a buttered baking sheet in a ring, leaving a space in the middle about 2½ inches in diameter. Use a teaspoon to make smaller ovals on top of the first layer. Repeat the procedure with the remaining dough, to make 2 rings. Brush the gougères with the milk and sprinkle each one with 2 tablespoons coarsely grated cheese. Bake in a preheated oven (375°) for about 45 minutes, or until they are well puffed and golden brown.

Serves 8 to 12.

Hot Water Hoecake

I don't know why these are so good. They're nothing really, but I guess it's the combination of crispness on the outside and the nutty cornmeal flavor on the inside and that little dab of cold butter— ummmm!

❧

1 cup white cornmeal
½ teaspoon salt
2¾ cups boiling water

1 tablespoon melted butter
(optional)

Add salt to cornmeal. Pour boiling water over all. Mix and let set for a few minutes. (Cornmeal will swell.) Drop batter from tip of cooking spoon on hot greased or buttered griddle or skillet (or the blade of your hoe, if you're a purist). Let brown on one side until edges are brown and crisp. Turn over and brown on other side until edges are crisp. Serve right away with cold dab of butter on each hot hoecake.

This should serve 6—count on 4.

For
Openers

I have a lot of different teasers like these because of the land office business done at DINAH'S BAR & GRILL during the cocktail—after tennis—post meetings—name your mission—hour.

Chicken Wings

2 dozen chicken wings	1 teaspoon monosodium glutamate
1 loaf stale, unsliced bread	½ teaspoon black pepper (if you
¾ cup Parmesan or Romano	like it hotter, add a few red
cheese, grated	pepper flakes or a dash of
¼ cup parsley, chopped	cayenne)
2 teaspoons salt	1 cup butter, melted
1 clove garlic, crushed	

Remove the crust from the loaf of bread. Grate it into crumbs, using the coarse side of the grater. Spread the crumbs out in a pan overnight to dry. Mix 2 cups crumbs with ¾ cup Parmesan or Romano cheese. Add parsley, salt, garlic, monosodium glutamate and pepper. Dip each chicken wing into butter and then into the crumb mixture. Be sure each piece is well coated. Lay the pieces in a shallow open roasting pan. I use a cookie pan. Pour the remaining butter over all the chicken wings and bake in a 350° oven about 30 or 40 minutes, until fork-tender. Do not turn chicken, but baste frequently with what drippings are in the pan.

Serves 10 as an hors d'oeuvre.

For a main course dinner dish, use 2 disjointed frying chickens instead of the chicken wings, and increase baking time to one hour. Or, if you like, you can use drumsticks for easy handling at buffet or dinner and bake 30 to 40 minutes. Try not to overcook.

Plan on 2 fryers serving 4 to 6 people, while 2 dozen drumsticks should handle 8 people unless you're a brilliant success, in which case it won't be nearly enough.

They're good cold the next day too.

Chicken or Turkey Water Chestnut Balls

Mix together as follows:

2 cups chopped leftover chicken or turkey (dark meat will do)

3 coarsely chopped water chestnuts

1 teaspoon grated onion

Dash of powdered ginger

Pinch of monosodium glutamate

Dash of black pepper

1 tablespoon soy sauce (this is your salt substitute here)

⅛ teaspoon powdered mustard

Make a very thick béchamel sauce as follows:

3 tablespoons butter

3 slices of onion

3 tablespoons flour

2 cups hot chicken broth

1 teaspoon soy sauce (to taste)

Dash of cayenne

Dash of powdered ginger

Dash of monosodium glutamate

Sauté the onion slices in butter. Lift out onion. Discard. It was only for flavor. Add flour, stir until smooth; add hot chicken broth, stirring until very smooth. Add soy sauce (instead of salt), cayenne, powdered ginger and monosodium glutamate.

Add the béchamel sauce to the chicken or turkey mixture, mix well, spread mixture in a flat dish or pie pan and set in refrigerator overnight (or for a couple of hours if you don't have that much time). Just before serving, taste for seasoning, correct, and roll into 1-inch balls. Roll in beaten egg to which 1 tablespoon of water has been added. Then roll in fresh bread crumbs, then again in egg and again in fresh bread crumbs. The moment your guests arrive, place the balls in very hot fat to cover (deep fat fry). Don't put too many in at once. Handle carefully and remove from fat when they are golden brown. Place on paper toweling to drain. Serve immediately.

I put them on a little plate. Serve only a few at a time, and in the center have a small container of hot catsup with a tiny dab of hot mustard sauce made from powdered mustard and cold water. If you have a large crowd coming, fry up a few ahead of time. Put them in a warm oven on paper toweling until you're ready to serve. Just be sure they stay crisp on the outside and moist on the inside.

Yields 12 to 14 balls. Figure two to a customer.

Quesadillas

This is a Mexican pizza of sorts and it's quick, easy and infallible. You can buy the thin tortillas at any supermarket. I prefer corn tortillas to the flour variety.

❧

3 corn or flour tortillas
½ cup Sharp Cheddar cheese, coarsely grated
½ cup Jack or Muenster cheese, coarsely grated
Salsa de Jalapèna or a Mexican hot-styled tomato sauce. (These are easy to get in Southern California. If you have any difficulty, you may substitute tomato sauce to which you've added a few drops of Tabasco.)

Brush sauce thinly over surface of tortillas. Sprinkle a mixture of the grated cheeses heavily over them. Bake in a preheated 400° oven on a cookie sheet until cheese is melted and tortillas are crisp. Cut into wedges and serve immediately with a cold drink.
    Serves 6.

Mushrooms and Sour Cream

1 pound small, fresh mushrooms
½ cube of butter
1 small onion, sliced
1 pint of sour cream
Salt and pepper

Clean mushrooms. Rinse lightly (don't soak, please). Dry well. Slice stems and all in halves or quarters, depending on size. Melt butter in a large skillet over medium heat. Sauté onions lightly until transparent. Add mushrooms and sauté until lightly browned. Add salt and pepper to taste, and sour cream. Turn heat on low, stirring until mushrooms and sour cream are heated through.

Serve with crisply toasted and buttered triangles of rye or white bread.

Serves 6.

Mushrooms and Sweet Cream

From the Spyros and Valerie Skouras kitchen. But beautiful!

❧

5 pounds mushrooms
½ pound butter
1 2-ounce jar pimentos
1 large green pepper, finely minced

2 tablespoons flour
Salt and pepper
1 pint thin cream

Pick small fresh mushrooms. Just rinse them. Don't soak in water to clean—they drink it all up and in the first step you'll just have a pan full of water. Brown mushrooms in butter. Then add pimentos, green pepper, flour, salt, pepper and cream. Cook for ½ hour.

Serve with crisp buttered thin toast and a little plate and fork— the sauce is too good for just a toothpick.

Serves 10 to 12 as an hors d'oeuvre.

This one may be used as an accompaniment to your entrée, in which case it will serve 6 to 8.

Pauline's Baked Mushrooms

This is another marvelous mushroom hors d'oeuvre.

❂

16 very large mushrooms
½ cup blanched almonds
1 cup leftover cooked meat
   or chicken
½ cup dry bread crumbs
4 green onions
2 medium-sized celery stalks

4 tablespoons butter
Salt to taste
Pepper to taste
Garlic powder to taste
Meat stock or gravy to moisten
   (about 1 cup)
Parsley, freshly chopped

Clean mushrooms. Rinse lightly. Don't soak. Separate the caps and the stems. Put the stems through the meat grinder with the almonds, cooked meat, green onion and celery. Melt the butter in skillet and add ground mixture. Sauté for about 7 or 8 minutes. Add the bread crumbs, salt, pepper, garlic powder and stir. Add the meat stock or gravy until all is moist. Cook slowly for another 2 minutes. Remove from heat and cool slightly. Stuff mushrooms with this mixture. Place them in a shallow baking pan and bake in a 350° oven for 20 or 25 minutes.

Serve these very hot with a sprinkling of chopped parsley on each one.

Serves 8 to 10.

Japanese Shrimp

I first had something like the following at the International Hotel in Las Vegas in their lovely little Japanese-type restaurant—and it's really simple and delicious. I have been in Japan twice and I have never found anyone in Japan who knows about this recipe or who has tasted it. I sincerely hope some day—in exchange for all those radios, television sets, cameras, etc., etc.—that I can export to the Nipponese people this recipe for Japanese Shrimp.

〰

1 pound medium-sized fresh green
    shrimp (approximately 1
    dozen), deveined and shelled
¼ cup Japanese shoyu sauce
    (soy sauce)
Juice of 1 lemon
1 lemon, sliced

¼ cup sweet sake (optional), a
    Japanese wine made from rice
2 tablespoons butter, or
    more if you like
¼ cup sesame seeds
Oil
2 tablespoons parsley, chopped

Oil griddle and then wipe it off. Lay shrimp in a symmetrical pattern (this will make it easier to slice them into bite-sized pieces right on the griddle). Grill the shrimp until they are pink on one side. This takes about 1½ minutes. Turn them over with a long spatula. Squeeze juice of 1 lemon over them. Add the lemon slices to the griddle (take the seeds out) and pour shoyu sauce over the whole thing. Now take a sharp knife and try to slice the shrimp (holding them down with a spatula or fork) into bite-sized pieces quickly and perfectly (good luck!). Add butter, a little more shoyu sauce—if you need it, and the sweet sake. Sprinkle the sesame seeds over the whole thing.

Have your serving dish warming in the oven. Don't let the shrimp overcook—I'd say 4 or 5 minutes at most. Move the shrimp around in the sauce so that it is completely coated. Sprinkle parsley over all before serving. Dish up and serve instantly.

Serves 3 to 4 people as an hors d'oeuvre, depending on how hungry they are and how long you intend to wait to serve the rest of the dinner.

I suggest you use your pancake griddle because for some reason the sauce gets a little thicker than it does in a large cast iron skillet.

Florentine Grilled Shrimp

Take 1 dozen fresh, green shrimp, peeled and deveined, but with the tails left on—you need them for dipping. Melt a cube of butter with 1 clove crushed garlic in a little skillet or small attractive saucepan. Brush shrimp lightly with garlic butter and sprinkle with salt and pepper. Grill on charcoal or under broiler, close to flame, quickly, turning when pink. Brush with garlic butter. When other side is finished, brush with more butter.

Serve shrimp on heat-proof dish around the little skillet or saucepan in which butter and garlic mixture was heated. Dip the shrimp in the garlic butter. Avoid close conversation with nonpartakers for a few hours.

Serves 4 to 6.

Shrimp Balls

1 pound raw shrimp, shelled, deveined and chopped medium fine	½ 5-oz. can water chestnuts, drained and chopped
1 slice thick bacon, diced	1½ teaspoons chopped onions
1 egg lightly beaten	1 teaspoon salt
1½ teaspoons cornstarch	Pinch ground ginger
2 cups oil	¼ teaspoon pepper

Combine all the ingredients except the oil in a bowl and chill. Just before serving, heat the oil in a skillet or deep fat fryer to 350°. Drop the shrimp mixture from a teaspoon (1 teaspoon at a time) in the hot oil. Cook, turning with tongs, until shrimp balls turn pink—no longer! It should take about 2 minutes. Drain on paper towels and serve very hot with a cocktail sauce.

Serves 6 to 8.

Cocktail Sauce

1 cup chili sauce or catsup	Dash Worcestershire
2 teaspoons horseradish	Dash Tabasco

Shrimp Arnaud

2 pounds cooked shrimp, peeled
5 green onions, chopped very fine,
    tops and all
¼ cup Dijon mustard
3 tablespoons prepared regula)
    mustard
3 tablespoons horseradish
Juice of 1 lemon

2 cloves garlic
1½ tablespoons paprika
1 teaspoon salt
¼ teaspoon pepper
¼ teaspoon red pepper flakes
1 teaspoon chervil leaves
1 teaspoon tarragon leaves
¾ cup olive oil

Mash garlic cloves. Place in oil, over night if possible. In mortar and pestle crush chervil and tarragon leaves. Mix all ingredients together. Marinate shrimp in mixture. Let set in refrigerator for at least 3 hours. One half hour before serving remove from refrigerator. Serve with little plates and forks—or with toothpicks.

    Serves 8 to 10 as an hors d'oeuvre, 6 as a first course.

Shrimp and Crab Buccaneer

3 pounds white crab meat, free
    of membranes
1½ pounds cooked shrimp, diced
2 hard cooked eggs, chopped
1½ green bell peppers, chopped
1 teaspoon freshly grated
    horseradish

1½ onions, chopped
2 tablespoons Worcestershire sauce
1 teaspoon dry mustard
½ teaspoon salt
1 teaspoon Tabasco
2 tablespoons sherry
½ cup fine cracker or bread crumbs

In a mixing bowl, combine crab meat, shrimp, eggs, green peppers and onions. Add horseradish, Worcestershire sauce, dry mustard, salt, Tabasco and sherry. Blend all the ingredients thoroughly. Chill.

    Roll mixture into small egg-shaped croquettes. This should yield about 20. Roll the croquettes lightly in cracker meal and fry them in deep hot fat (350°) to a rich golden brown. Drain well and serve with tartar or seafood cocktail sauce.

    Serves 10 to 12.

    As a main dish, divide into 8 parts and it should serve 8.

Chopped Chicken Liver

I got this recipe many years ago from my roommate at the time, Kitty Kallen. We shared expenses while she sang for Jimmy Dorsey and I sang for Eddie Cantor. We also shared clothes and recipes. She gave me a great one for marinated herring and this one for chopped chicken livers. If that sounds illogical coming from somebody named Kitty Kallen, please know that this is as authentic as it is illogical.

1 pound chicken livers
4 hard-boiled eggs
1 hard-boiled egg (for garnish)

2 onions, finely chopped or grated
1 teaspoon sugar (optional)

Boil livers until just done. In a wooden chopping bowl, chop the livers, 4 eggs, and onions together while livers and eggs are still hot—this makes them blend better. Add enough chicken fat or butter to make smooth. Season with salt and pepper. If the livers are a little bitter, add a teaspoon of sugar. Boil an extra egg with which to decorate the top. Separate the white from the yolk, grate on a fine grater, and sprinkle the grated egg over the top.
 Serves 8.

Big Deal Chopped Chicken Liver or Chicken Liver Paté

1 pound chicken livers
2 medium onions, chopped
¾ cup butter
1 clove garlic, mashed
1 tablespoon flour
¼ teaspoon sugar
1 teaspoon salt
½ teaspoon pepper
1 bay leaf

Pinch of thyme
Pinch of oregano
Pinch of tarragon
3 tablespoons brandy
Clarified sweet butter (to clarify,
    melt slowly and let all sediment
    settle to bottom—what remains
    on top is clarified butter)

Sauté onions in ½ cup butter with garlic until just tender. Remove from skillet. Add ¼ cup butter and sauté livers until almost tender. Sprinkle with flour and stir in salt, pepper, bay leaf, thyme, oregano and tarragon. Cover and simmer for 1 minute over very low heat. Remove bay leaf. Cool slightly and combine with sautéed onions. At this point use a blender if possible. Put livers, etc., in blender a little at a time; add brandy gradually. If no blender, use meat grinder with fine blade and put through 3 times. Then add brandy and taste for seasoning.

To assemble and garnish: Let liver paté cool to room temperature. Pour into attractive serving bowl or wide-mouthed crock or pottery jar. Cover with thin coating of the clarified butter and refrigerate. To seal more permanently, a thicker coating of clarified butter should be used. Do not freeze.

Serves 8.

Sicilian Eggplant Caponata

1 large (or 2 small) eggplant, peeled and diced into 1-inch cubes
½ cup olive oil
2 onions, thinly sliced
1 cup celery, diced
2 cups Italian canned tomatoes (a 16-ounce can)

2 tablespoons capers, drained
1 tablespoon pignolas (pine nuts)
8 or 10 black Italian olives, pitted and coarsely chopped
2 tablespoons sugar
¼ cup wine vinegar
½ teaspoon salt
Dash of pepper

Heat olive oil in frying pan and fry the eggplant until it is softened and browned on all sides. Remove pieces to a saucepan. Add onions to frying pan, adding a little more oil if necessary, and sauté the slices until they are soft and golden, taking care not to burn them. Add celery, then canned tomatoes that have been forced through a strainer or blended in a blender. Simmer the onions, celery and tomatoes together for 15 minutes. Add the drained capers, pine nuts and olives.

In a small saucepan over low heat, dissolve the sugar in wine vinegar and add salt and a good dash of pepper. Combine all the above ingredients with the eggplant. Cover the pan and allow the mixture barely to simmer over very low heat for 20 minutes to blend the flavors. Let the caponata cool and chill it in the refrigerator before serving. Serve with crusty Italian bread.

This will keep for a while in your refrigerator—if you have any left. Serves 8 to 10.

Herring Salad

Nice for a longer-than-usual cocktail hour.

1 can (5½ ounces) Swedish matjes herring
2 cups boiled potatoes, diced
2 cups pickled beets, diced
⅔ cup sweet pickle, diced
1 cup tart apple, diced

¼ teaspoon white pepper
¼ cup onion, finely chopped
2 tablespoons red wine vinegar
2 tablespoons water
2 tablespoons sugar
1 cup thick sour cream

Drain herring thoroughly and dice. Combine it with the potatoes, beets, sweet pickle, apple and onion. Blend the vinegar, water and sugar together. Add to the mixture, stirring all carefully.

Fold in the sour cream and pack the mixture into a mold or a bowl which has first been rinsed with cold water. Chill very thoroughly, at least 2 hours.

Unmold the herring salad onto a flat round dish or platter and garnish with a ring of parsley. Serve with additional sour cream in a separate bowl, and buttered thin slices of rye bread.

Serves 12.

Steak Tartare

I don't eat rare hamburger or steak—it has to be medium "toward the well"—but I love steak tartare. You figure it!

In Honolulu I once had this served with a layer of mayonnaise over the top of the steak "loaf," a layer of chopped green peppers over the mayonnaise, and on top of that a layer of chopped salted tomatoes—a really fabulous combination of flavors and textures for some reason. Serve with thin buttered toasted rye or pumpernickel slices.

❀

2 pounds choice or prime ground sirloin	Worcestershire sauce (to taste)
2 tablespoons capers	Dash Tabasco
1 small onion, chopped	Black pepper (a lot)
2 tablespoons olive oil	1 tablespoon red wine vinegar
Salt, to taste	2 egg yolks
6 anchovy filets, cut in small pieces	¼ cup chopped parsley
	½ teaspoon prepared mustard (Dijon, preferably)

Mix ingredients carefully to retain fluffiness. Shape in large loaf. Garnish with anchovy strips, more onions, more capers. May be cooked if the thought of raw meat turns you off.

Serves 8 to 10.

Steak or Chicken Teriyaki

1½ pounds filet mignon or sirloin steak *or*

2 uncooked chicken breasts, boned

Cut filet mignon or sirloin into ¼ inch slices after removing fat and gristle. If you use chicken breasts, cut into bit-sized chunks. Marinate the beef or chicken chunks in the Teriyaki sauce (see below) for about 15 to 20 minutes. Cook over hot charcoal grill or under the broiler for about 2 to 3 minutes on each side, brushing with marinade before and after you turn it. (You can skewer the meat. Alternate chicken with pineapple chunks and even a scallion—if you like—on the skewer.) Place on a warm dish; sprinkle a little glaze (recipe below) over each piece and serve immediately.

Teriyaki Sauce or Marinade

1 cup Mirin (cooking sake) or 1 cup dry sherry (scant)

1 cup shoyu or soy sauce
1 cup chicken broth

Heat sake or sherry in saucepan. Light a match to it—it will flame. Shake back and forth until flame goes out. Add soy sauce and chicken broth and let come to a boil. Remove to a medium-sized mixing bowl to let it cook.

Glaze

¼ cup of cooled sauce or marinade
2 teaspoons cornstarch
1 teaspoon sugar

Take the cooled sauce and add the sugar and cornstarch dissolved in 1 tablespoon water. Heat all together over low heat, stirring constantly until it becomes a syrupy glaze.

The sauce can be saved in the refrigerator if tightly covered for three or four weeks. Just bring to a boil before using and let cool. You won't have any of the glaze left over so don't worry about it.

Serves 6 to 8.

Pauline's Deviled Egg Salad

This has a few twists to the plot that would do credit to a Hitchcock movie. Just when you think you've got the bacon or pickles pegged, you bite into a tantalizing little something else—pray it isn't a piece of egg shell.

6 hard-boiled eggs, chopped
2 sweet pickles, chopped
3 slices bacon, fried crisp and crumbled

Salt to taste
Pepper, freshly ground, to taste
Mayonnaise to moisten

Combine ingredients and fold into mayonnaise. Spread between slices of thinly sliced bread, or serve open-faced. Trim crusts and cut into strips or triangles.

Yields enough for 6 open-faced sandwiches.

Extra Ideas

I make Meat Balls out of the Meat Loaf recipe on page 62. Brown on all sides in a little oil. Serve as an hors d'oeuvre with a toothpick.

The Goujonnettes of Sole with Tartar Sauce on page 85 are great for the cocktail hour. Just use one-half of the amount and slice in thinner strips before following directions.

Also, Sausage and Peppers on page 79. I cut them in bite-sized pieces and serve them on toothpicks or skewers.

Buttered Tiny Thin Biscuits with Country Fried Ham

This is better than anything in the world—well, almost.

❧

Bake biscuits about 1½ inches in diameter from Biscuit recipe on page 23.   Take sliced squares of country ham (cut approximately the same size as the biscuit), which you have fried in a little butter, and place between the hot, split, buttered biscuits.

20 small biscuits—should serve 10 people

Soups

Many times when I have an especially good soup dish I serve it in the living room before dinner. For hot soups I use a large tureen and soup cups—for cold ones I use a punch bowl or salad bowl and cups. Just ladle it out—it's pretty and easy to handle. It shortens a sometimes interminable cocktail hour when somebody is late in arriving. Also, nobody is embarrassed at asking for seconds. It's obvious whether or not there are any.

Pauline's Onion Soup

4 large onions, thinly sliced	6 cups hot beef consommé
¼ cup butter	Slices of sour dough bread, toasted
1 tablespoon flour	Parmesan cheese, grated

Sauté the onions in butter until lightly browned. Add the flour and stir until well blended. Gradually add the hot consommé, stirring vigorously until blended with the flour and butter mixture. Bring to a boil and simmer for 5 minutes.

Serve in individual soup bowls with a thick slice of sour dough bread, toasted in the oven for extra crispness, floating on top. Sprinkle Parmesan cheese over the top.

Serves 6.

Fresh Pea Soup

1 package frozen peas or	3 tablespoons barley
1 pound fresh peas shelled —	Pinch of basil
save 3 or 4 shells	Sprigs of mint
1 cup chicken broth	1 small onion
	1 stalk celery

Cook peas with celery, a small onion and 3 or 4 shells in a little broth until just done. Remove onion, celery and shells. Place peas in a blender with lump of butter, a little broth, milk, a tiny pinch of basil, and fresh mint if you can get it.

Meanwhile, in remaining broth cook 3 tablespoons barley until just done. When soup is blended and barley is done, drain barley and add to soup (adding milk if necessary). Soup should not be too thick. Heat and serve with tiny crisp fried croutons and a sprinkle of mint (very, very little). I've been a smash with this one!

I use barley, but I had a pea soup in Lucerne, Switzerland, once where they had boiled a little vermicelli al dente and mixed that with it. It was delicious.

Serves 4.

Pumpkin Soup

My producer has a will of iron. He insisted I cook pumpkin soup for Vincent Price when he appeared on our Halloween show. I protested because pumpkin soup has always sounded pretty unappealing to me. He looked at me in astonishment. "Are you," he asked, "one of those obstinates who refuses to try something just because you don't like the sound of it?"

Fade out, fade in. I cooked pumpkin soup for Vincent Price on the Halloween show....

I served it at no less than three dinner parties at home during the week following the show. It's that delicious. The moral? Take a chance and listen to your producer.

❀

4 tablespoons butter
4 scallions, chopped
1 small onion, sliced
1½ pounds pumpkin, peeled
    and diced
4 cups chicken stock

½ teaspoon salt
2 tablespoons flour
¾ cup hot light cream
Tiny toasted croutons
Whipped cream, slightly salted

Melt 2 tablespoons butter in a large saucepan. Add scallions and onion slices and cook them gently until they are almost soft but not brown. Add pumpkin, chicken stock and salt. Simmer until pumpkin is soft. Stir in flour kneaded with 1 tablespoon butter and bring the soup to a boil. Press the soup through a fine sieve or purée it in a blender. Correct the seasoning and add the light cream and 1 tablespoon butter. Heat the soup just to the boiling point and serve it garnished with the tiny toasted croutons and whipped cream.

Spinach Soup

While we were testing recipes for this book everybody within eating distance gained a little. On one particular evening Anne and Kirk Douglas carried what was left over of this soup home in a doggie bag (jar?). Kirk rated it G.P. The prune whip for dessert he rated X—too good for kids. (See Prune Whip recipe on page 160. But first try the Spinach Soup.)

❀

⅓ cup green onions or yellow
   onions, minced
3 tablespoons butter
4 cups packed with spinach leaves,
   cut into very thin slices
   or shreds
½ teaspoon salt
½ teaspoon pepper

3 tablespoons flour
5½ cups white chicken stock or
   canned chicken broth (if broth
   is not strong, add 2 cubes
   chicken bouillon to the broth)
2 egg yolks
½ cup whipping cream

Wash spinach leaves and dry in a towel. Cook onions slowly in 3 tablespoons of butter in a covered saucepan for 5 to 10 minutes until tender, but not brown. Stir in the spinach leaves and salt and pepper. Cover and cook slowly for about 5 minutes or until the leaves are tender and wilted. Sprinkle in the flour and stir over moderate heat for 3 minutes. Lift pan off the burner. Beat in boiling chicken stock or chicken broth. Return pan to burner and simmer for 5 minutes. Correct for seasoning.

If not to be served immediately, set aside uncovered. Reheat to simmer before proceeding

Blend the egg yolks and whipping cream in a mixing bowl. Beat 1 cup of hot soup into the egg and cream mixture very, very slowly. Gradually beat in the rest of the soup in a thin stream. Return the soup to the saucepan. Stir over low to moderate heat for a minute or two, but do not bring soup to a simmer. Remove saucepan from burner. Pour soup into a tureen or soup cups and decorate with a sprig of watercress.

To serve cold: If the soup is too thick, stir in a little more cream before serving.

Serves 8.

Navy Bean Soup

2 cups white beans
Ham bone with some lean
    meat on it or
a ¼ to ½ lb. piece of ham
3 onions, chopped fine
1 bunch of celery, tops included,
    chopped fine

Clove of garlic, finely chopped
1 tomato, chopped
Parsley, finely chopped
½ cup cooked mashed potatoes
3 quarts of water
Salt and pepper to taste

Put the beans, which have been soaked over night, into a soup kettle with the ham bone and cover with 3 quarts of water. Cook very slowly; after a couple of hours, or when beans are half cooked, add the mashed potatoes. Stir until thoroughly mixed. Then add onions, tomato, celery, garlic and parsley. After soup has begun to boil, turn the fire low and let simmer for about an hour. Then remove the ham bone; chop up all pieces of meat on it and return the meat to soup before serving.
    Serves 8.

Quick Purée Mongol

1 can tomato soup
1 can pea soup or 1 package
    frozen peas
1 soup can of milk

¼ cup dry sherry
1 stalk celery cut in julienne slivers
1 carrot, cut in julienne slivers

If you use frozen peas, cook peas as directed on package; drain and put through the blender with a little milk. Then return to saucepan. Add tomato soup, milk and the julienned vegetables. Cover and let simmer over low flame for about 30 minutes to blend. 10 minutes before serving add ¼ cup dry sherry; let heat through again. Salt and pepper generously and serve with crisply fried croutons.
    If you use the canned pea soup, simply add it to the tomato soup and milk and follow above procedure.
    Serves 4 to 6.

Minestrone

My minestrone, as you may notice, is simply a heavy vegetable soup. With crusty French or Italian bread, green salad and a nice cheese, it's all you'd want for a great wintertime dinner.

❧

4 carrots	2-inch wedge cabbage
4 stalks celery (with leaves)	1 onion
1 leek	1 clove garlic
1 small bunch parsley	2 teaspoons salt
1 can kidney beans	2 tomatoes (or ½ can)
1 teaspoon minced basil	1 tablespoon olive oil
½ teaspoon pepper	Parmesan cheese, grated
2 packages frozen lima beans (optional)	2 packages frozen corn (optional)
	½ cup barley
Ham or beef for stock	½ cup macaroni
2 potatoes	

Wash and prepare the vegetables: carrots, potatoes, cabbage and garlic go into the pot whole, while the onion, parsley, leek and celery should be coarsely chopped. Bring to boil and simmer for 1 hour in a large pot with 2 quarts of water and the salt.

Take the potato masher and mash all the vegetables. Add the beans, cut-up tomatoes, basil, olive oil, pepper, corn and lima beans. Give the soup another hour to cook and then turn it into a tureen. With each bowl pass a dish of grated cheese and warm, crusty Italian or French bread.

Total cooking time is 2½ hours.

Serves 8.

Mother's Borscht

10 large beets, peeled and grated	4 tablespoons sugar
2½ quarts water	¾ cup lemon juice
1 onion, minced	2 eggs
1½ teaspoons salt	1 cup sour cream

Combine beets, water, onion and salt in a saucepan. Bring to a boil and cook over low heat for 1 hour. Add sugar and lemon juice. Cook 10 minutes and taste to correct seasoning. Beat eggs in a bowl. Gradually add to the soup, stirring steadily to prevent curdling. Chill. Taste for seasoning. You may have to add much more sugar and lemon juice—but do it gradually, tasting all the time. Just before serving stir in sour cream, first adding some of the soup to the cream so that it will blend more readily.

Serve with cold cubed boiled potatoes if you like. Garnish with a dab of sour cream and a little sprinkle of fresh dill if it's available—if not, chopped parsley. One country club out here serves this in tall beautiful parfait glasses for luncheons and it's as pretty as it is delicious. If your guests want to drink it, leave out little surprises like the boiled potatoes and the dab of sour cream.

Serves 8.

Gazpacho

This is another great summer soup.

❧

1 cucumber (small)	2 tablespoons mild vinegar
1 medium onion	Juice of ½ lemon or more
2 large tomatoes	(don't get it too sour)
1 clove garlic	5 tablespoons cooking oil
¼ green pepper	2 teaspoons salt
½ cup sour cream	½ teaspoon pepper
1 egg yolk	Fresh peppercorns
1 teaspoon paprika	

Chop vegetables coarsely; place with all other ingredients into blender. Run at high speed until of very smooth consistency. If too thick, add another half-tomato. Taste to make sure you have enough salt, etc. Chill thoroughly; serve in chilled soup bowls accompanied with a condiment tray of one dish of finely chopped onions, one dish of finely chopped tomatoes, one dish of finely chopped cucumbers, and small toasted croutons. The diner selects his own garnishes.

Serves 4.

Potage Senegalese (Iced Chicken and Curry Soup)

2 tablespoons butter
1 onion, finely chopped
1 small apple, sliced
2 teaspoons good curry powder
4 tablespoons flour
½ cup frozen cooked peas, puréed
1½ cups cream

Salt
Chili pepper
Cayenne pepper
3 cups strong chicken stock
  or broth
½ cup chicken breast, finely diced

Melt butter in pan. Add onion and apple slices and cook very slowly until quite soft without browning. Add flour and curry powder and cook slowly for another 5 to 6 minutes. Stir in cayenne pepper and chili pepper. Stir in the stock until smooth. Add purée of cooked peas. Stir over the heat until the soup comes to a boil. Rub through a fine strainer. Chill thoroughly or if you've run out of time, stir over ice until very cold. Add the cream and diced chicken. If possible, serve in small bowls surrounded by crushed ice. This is good served hot, too.
    Serves 6.

Cold Cucumber Soup

1 clove garlic, finely chopped
½ teaspoon salt
2 cups cucumbers, finely chopped
1 cup cooked beets, chopped
4 cups sour cream

1 cup milk
2 teaspoons parsley, chopped
2 teaspoons chives, chopped
Salt and pepper to taste

Chop the garlic with the salt and mix thoroughly with the cucumbers and cooked beets. Add the sour cream, milk, parsley and chives. Salt and pepper to taste. Chill and serve in soup cups with a thin slice of unpeeled cucumber and a dab of sour cream.
    Serves 6.

The Main Dish

Meats

Fish and Shellfish

Poultry—Chicken, Duckling and Turkey

Casseroles and One-Dish Meals

Cheese, Rice, Pasta and Potatoes

Vegetables

Meats

Beef Stroganoff and Kasha

4 lbs. top sirloin sliced in thin
    strips, fat and gristle removed
4 onions, chopped fine
2 cloves garlic, crushed
1 lb. fresh mushrooms, sliced
2 cups chicken or beef broth
4 tablespoons flour

2 pints sour cream
2 tablespoons Worcestershire sauce
Paprika
Pepper
Fresh dill if you can find it
Chopped parsley

Sauté the onions and garlic in butter until they are glazed and lightly browned. This should take about 7 minutes. Add sliced mushrooms (caps and stems). Sauté a few minutes longer (3 or 4 minutes should do it). Remove the vegetables to a hot platter and place in a warm oven. Add a little more butter if needed. Season your beef with salt and pepper generously and toss in a paper bag in which you have put about ½ cup of flour. You may need more. The beef should be lightly floured, but thoroughly coated. Brown meat over high heat on each side, turning only once. Remove the meat when it is brown to the hot vegetable platter. Add more butter to the drippings if needed. Blend the 4 tablespoons of flour with the drippings remaining in the pan.

Meanwhile, bring the broth to a boil, add all at once to the butter and flour mixture, stirring vigorously until the sauce is thickened and smooth. Add the sour cream. Turn heat very low, stirring constantly so that the sour cream will not curdle. Add the Worcestershire sauce and sprinkle with paprika and pepper. Add the beef and vegetables to the sauce and heat through. Taste for seasoning. Serve over steamed Kasha and sprinkle a little chopped fresh dill and/or parsley over top.

Serves 8 to 10.

Kasha

2 cups whole roasted buckwheat groats	2 cups chicken or beef broth
2 eggs	Salt
	2 tablespoons butter

Mix the eggs with the buckwheat groats. Put in a heated, heavy saucepan for which you have a good cover. Stir until each groat is separate. Add 2 cups of broth to the mixture. Cover tightly, turn heat very low and steam for 30 minutes. Just before serving, add salt and butter.

Brisket of Beef with Puréed Vegetable Gravy

3 or 4 pounds fairly lean brisket of beef	3 tomatoes, peeled and coarsely chopped
1 onion, coarsely chopped	Salt and pepper to taste
4 stalks celery, coarsely chopped	½ cup red wine
½ green pepper, coarsely chopped	½ cup beef broth
3 carrots, coarsely chopped	

Season brisket of beef generously with salt and pepper. Brown meat on both sides in hot oil or butter in a Dutch oven. Remove meat and place vegetables on bottom of Dutch oven and replace meat on top. Cover and bake for 2 hours in a preheated 300° oven, occasionally basting with juices from the meat. Add wine and beef broth. Uncover and bake until meat is tender.

Make a gravy by puréeing the cooked vegetables and adding to the broth remaining in Dutch oven, after first skimming off excess fat. Serve with Kasha or Potato Pancakes or potatoes cut in half, roasted and basted with the meat for the last hour of cooking.

Serves 6 to 8.

Pauline's Corned Beef and Cabbage

4 to 5 pounds corned beef brisket
1 clove garlic
2 whole cloves
10 whole black peppers
2 bay leaves
1 pound string beans, with ends
    trimmed (optional but
    beautiful)

8 medium carrots, pared
8 medium potatoes, pared
8 medium yellow onions
1 medium cabbage,
    cut into wedges
2 tablespoons butter or margarine
Chopped parsley
Mustard Sauce or Cream Mustard

Wipe corned beef with damp paper towels. Place in large kettle; cover with cold water. Add garlic, cloves, black peppers, bay leaves. Bring to a boil. Reduce heat; simmer 5 minutes. Skim surface. Cover kettle; simmer 3 to 4 hours, or until corned beef is fork-tender. Add carrots, potatoes, onions and string beans during the last 25 minutes (each tied in cheese cloth to stay separate and whole while cooking). Add cabbage wedges during the last 15 minutes. Cook vegetables until just tender. Slice corned beef thinly across the grain. Arrange slices on platter with cabbage. Brush potatoes with butter; sprinkle with parsley. Serve with Mustard Sauce, Cream Mustard or plain mustard.

    Serves 8.

Mustard Sauce

2 egg yolks
½ teaspoon dry mustard
1 teaspoon lemon juice
3 tablespoons Dijon mustard

1½ cups heavy cream
Salt
White pepper

Beat egg yolks with dry mustard. Add lemon juice slowly and beat until thick. Mix in Dijon mustard and trickle in the cream, stirring with a wooden spoon. Season with salt and pepper to taste. Refrigerate for 1 hour or more.

Cream Mustard

1 teaspoon prepared mustard
Salt
Pepper

Few drops lemon juice
¾ teaspoon Dijon mustard
½ cup heavy cream

Mix together prepared mustard, lemon juice, and Dijon mustard. Add heavy cream, plain or whipped, little by little, stirring vigorously until the sauce is well combined. Salt and pepper to taste.

Bill Holden's Marinated Hawaiian Steak

The reason I call this "Hawaiian" is that the first time we tasted it the Holdens were in Hawaii with their kids and George and I were over there with ours. The children were quite small. The steaks weren't. Bill cooked them himself. I don't know what other culinary talents he has—but he doesn't need too many more with a specialty like this going for him.

◆

6 1½-inch sirloin steaks

Hawaiian Sauce

1 cup Japanese shoyu sauce
or soya sauce
2 drops sugar substitute
1 heaping teaspoon fresh ginger
root, grated

½ teaspoon garlic powder
1 tablespoon cooking oil
1 tablespoon sesame seed
1 tablespoon sherry, bourbon
or brandy

Marinate steaks with sauce about 30 minutes to 1 hour before cooking over charcoal or under broiler.
Serves 6.

About Ground Meat

I am a ground meat lover. But I prefer it coarsely ground with a good solid texture that bites back. It seems to absorb seasonings more readily than chunk style. Whenever possible I use chuck instead of sirloin but I'm not all that partial. I like ground meat in almost any form — ground chuck, ground round, ground sirloin, ground veal, ground pork, ground chicken.

Here are some grand ground recipes:

Meat Loaf

2 pounds twice-ground beef	1 cup minced onion
2 pounds twice-ground pork	1 tablespoon salt
2 cups soft bread crumbs	¼ teaspoon black pepper
1 16-ounce can tomatoes	Consommé or beef broth
3 eggs, slightly beaten	3 tablespoons flour
2 tablespoons hot green peppers, minced	⅓ cup crisp bacon, crumbled
	4 strips uncooked bacon

Mix the first 8 ingredients and shape the mixture into a loaf on a shallow roasting pan. Lay strips of bacon over the loaf. Bake in a moderate oven (350°) about 1½ hours. Drain off the drippings and juices, adding enough consommé or beef broth to make 3 cups. Blend the flour with enough water to make a paste. Add to drippings and cook until it is smooth and thickened. Just before serving, add the crumbled bacon to the gravy.

Serves 8 to 10.

A variation: Make your favorite stuffed deviled egg recipe, using 4 eggs. Put filled egg halves together. Put half your meat loaf on bottom of pan. Lay stuffed eggs in a row down the center of the meat. Cover with rest of meat mixture. Mold into loaf around and over eggs. Bake as above.

Another variation: Shape into one-inch meat balls; fry and serve.

Hamburgers with Almonds

I got this recipe while I was singing one summer in Colorado Springs. The lady who books the acts, Carol Truax, also happens to be one of the world's great cooks and one of the few who isn't averse to giving out her recipes. She wrote the original Ladies' Home Journal Cookbook, *which is to my way of thinking the best one around.*

I don't remember if she gave me this one or if I filched it by watching. At any rate, that night I ate six hamburgers.

❧

2 pounds ground chuck	2 teaspoons fines herbes
1 5½-ounce package almonds, slivered or chopped lengthwise	1 teaspoon monosodium glutamate
	Salt and pepper to taste

Sprinkle almonds on a cookie sheet and toast in a preheated oven to crisp them. Be careful not to let them burn. Mix ground chuck, slivered almonds, fines herbs, and seasonings together. Don't handle the meat too much. Form into patties. Charcoal broil, or cook in a skillet with a little oil and butter as you would any other hamburgers.

Serve on a toasted, buttered hamburger bun. Don't put out any mustard, catsup, pickles or relish or anything else for these hamburgers, for somebody might use them and ruin the whole flavor and texture.

Serves 8.

Filled Hamburgers

Use round steak, ground chuck or a mixture

Take 2 smaller than regular size hamburger patties. Flatten between pieces of wax paper. Spread a little mustard on the bottom patty and catsup if you like it. Then put over the mustard 1 teaspoon of chopped fresh onion, 1 teaspoon pickled relish and 1 tablespoon grated sharp Cheddar cheese. Leave a little room on the outer edges of the hamburger. Place top patty over bottom and press outer edges together. Season with salt, pepper and monosodium glutamate.

Fry, grill or broil—but turn only once and carefully so that the filling stays in the hamburger.

Serve with or without a bun.

Serves 4 to 6 (using two pounds of meat).

Pepper Hamburger Steak

2 pounds ground beef, sirloin preferably
4 teaspoons black pepper, freshly ground
Salt
4 teaspoons butter
Tabasco sauce, to taste
1 tablespoon Worcestershire sauce
Parsley, chopped
Chives, chopped
2 tablespoons brandy, warmed, or red wine

Shape the beef lightly into four cakes and sprinkle each side with pepper. With the heel of the hand, press the pepper into the meat and let stand for about 30 minutes. Sprinkle a light layer of salt over the bottom of a heavy skillet, place over high heat and, when the salt begins to brown, add the hamburgers. Cook until well browned on one side. Turn and cook 30 seconds over high heat, then lower the heat to medium and cook for a couple of minutes for rare, a minute more for medium.

Sprinkle with a little lemon juice, Tabasco, Worcestershire. Remove patties to warm platter. Stir sauce in skillet. Add a little butter, a

couple tablespoons red wine, or brandy if you like. Turn heat up, pour over each patty. Sprinkle with finely chopped parsley and chives.
Serves 4.

Hamburger De Luxe

2 pounds lean round steak, ground	1 teaspoon salt (or to taste)
1 egg	¼ teaspoon pepper
1 teaspoon dry or English mustard	1 cup chicken broth or consommé
2 tablespoons Worcestershire sauce	2 medium-size onions, thinly sliced

Mix meat, eggs, seasonings thoroughly. Add consommé gradually, blending well. Shape into patties. Brown them quickly in fat and finish cooking over a low heat. Remove the hamburgers from the pan and keep them hot. Add onions to the fat in the pan. Sauté over a low heat until brown and serve on the side.
Serves 4.

Calves' Liver Veneziana

This has got to be good—it was the first thing Jody admitted he liked besides hamburgers, pizza, and cocoa-crunchy, sugar-coated crispy cereal!

❧

2 pounds calves' liver, thinly sliced crosswise or cut in strips	Flour
	1 tablespoon minced parsley
3 cups onions, thinly sliced	1 tablespoon beef bouillon
1¾ cups butter	Salt
¼ cup olive oil	Black pepper, freshly ground

Sauté onions in combined butter and olive oil for 15 minutes or until onions are lightly browned. Sprinkle liver with a little flour and season with salt and pepper. Add liver slices to onions and cook over high heat for 5 minutes. Add parsley and bouillon. Serve immediately.
Serves 6.

Brown Stock and Brown Sauce (Sauce Espagnole)

If you want beautifully browned, deeply flavored gravies and sauces like you find in good restaurants with your meat dishes, you really should use a few tablespoons or more (depending on the recipe) of Brown Sauce or Sauce Espagnole. It takes a few hours to make it, but it keeps a lot longer than that. As a matter of fact, it keeps well in the refrigerator for ten days or two weeks and in the freezer for about two months. It will be well worth the trouble you've gone through to make it and you'll have saved time in the long run. It may be that secret ingredient — that little something — "they" left out when "they" gave the recipe to you only because "they" have it on hand and "they" figure you don't. First you make a . . .

❀

Brown Stock

2 pounds meaty beef bones	1½ teaspoons salt
2 pounds veal bones	Pinch of thyme
2 onions, cubed	4 sprigs parsley
1 carrot, cubed	2 stalks celery
3 quarts cold water	1 small bay leaf

Crack bones into small pieces. Spread vegetables and bones out in a flat pan. Brown well on all sides in a moderately hot oven (375°). Transfer to a kettle and add cold water, salt, thyme, parsley, celery and bay leaf. Bring the water slowly to a boil, skimming the fat from the surface when necessary. Cook the stock slowly for at least 4 hours, adding more water if necessary. Strain the stock through a fine sieve or cheese-cloth.

Yields approximately 2½ quarts. **Then your . . .**

Brown Sauce (Sauce Espagnole) or Demi Glacé

½ cup beef, veal, or pork drippings	1 stalk celery
2 onions, coarsely chopped	1 small bay leaf
1 small carrot, coarsely chopped	1 garlic clove, crushed
½ cup flour	Pinch of thyme
8 cups hot brown stock	¼ cup tomato sauce or ½ cup tomato purée
3 sprigs parsley	

In a heavy saucepan melt the beef, veal or pork drippings. Add onions and carrot and cook them until the onions start to turn golden, shaking

66

the pan to ensure even cooking. Add flour and cook the mixture, stirring, until the flour, carrot and onions are a rich brown. Add 3 cups hot brown stock, parsley, celery, bay leaf, garlic and thyme and cook the mixture, stirring frequently, until it thickens. Add 3 more cups stock and simmer the sauce slowly, stirring occasionally, for 1 to 1½ hours, or until it is reduced about one-half. As it cooks, skim off the fat that rises to the surface. Add tomato sauce or tomato purée, cook the sauce for a few minutes more, and strain it through a fine sieve. Add 2 more cups stock and continue to cook the sauce slowly for about 1 hour, skimming the surface from time to time, until it is reduced to about 4 cups. Strain the sauce and let it cool.

Yields approximately 4 cups.

Veal Chasseur

2 pounds thin, thin veal cutlets, gristle and fat trimmed off
2 tablespoons butter
½ pound mushrooms, sliced
Juice of ½ lemon
3 tablespoons shallots
¾ cup dry white wine
¾ cup dry sherry
1 quart Brown Sauce
1 16-ounce can drained tomatoes or 3 peeled fresh large tomatoes

Sauté mushrooms in melted butter. Sprinkle lemon over all. Cook 2 or 3 minutes. Add two teaspoons of the shallots and the combined wines except for ¼ cup of the sherry. When liquid is reduced to one-third, lower heat and add 1 quart Brown Sauce. If sauce now appears too thin, dissolve 1 teaspoon cornstarch in a little cold water and add to sauce. Add the tomatoes and bring to a boil. Reduce heat and cook for another 10 minutes. If fresh tomatoes are used, add an extra 10 minutes for cooking. This part can be done in the morning and reheated before serving.

Salt and pepper the veal and dust lightly in flour and sauté quickly in hot butter for 2 minutes on each side. Place on a warm platter until sauce is ready. Add to the leavings in the pan a teaspoon of finely minced shallots and brown a little. Now add ¼ cup dry sherry, mix all together, heat through and pour over the veal on the warm platter. Serve immediately with steamed rice.

Serves 6.

Veal is very special—hard to come by—out in California anyway. Real veal has a whitish color. It's delicate and light and must never be overcooked. There are a hundred different ways to flavor and cook it. Here are just a few. I had a hard time making up my mind on which ones to use here. For the ones that got away, see the next book.

Veal Piccata

1½ pounds veal, cut into
    thin slices
Flour
Parmesan cheese
Salt to taste
Black pepper, freshly ground,
    to taste
Butter

Juice of 3 lemons, or more if
    needed
½ cup beef broth
¼ cup dry white wine
1 egg yolk, beaten
Parsley
Lemon slices

Lightly pound very thin veal even thinner between sheets of wax paper. Dip veal slices in a mixture of flour, Parmesan, salt and black pepper. Melt butter in a large skillet. Add the juice of 2 lemons to the butter. Sauté veal about 2 minutes on each side. Sprinkle more lemon juice over veal. Remove meat to hot platter and place in oven to keep warm.

Mix beaten egg yolk with a little broth and wine. Add remaining broth and wine to drippings in pan, scraping loose all the particles, and then add egg. Bring to a boil, stirring vigorously. Pour over veal and garnish with parsley and lemon slices.

Serves 4.

Veal Scaloppine with Cheese

1½ pounds veal cutlets
4 teaspoons butter
Fine fresh bread or cracker crumbs
1 egg

Salt and pepper
Swiss, Gruyère or Mozzarella
    cheese

Pound very thin veal cutlets thinner between 2 pieces of wax paper with flat side of mallet or cleaver. Beat egg with salt and pepper. Dip cutlets in egg, then in bread or cracker crumbs. Sauté slowly in butter until delicate brown.

Arrange in shallow baking dish. Cover with thin layer of cheese. Bake in preheated 375° oven until cheese is melted. This should be served right away, before cheese hardens. You may place a thin layer of Prosciutto on veal and then add cheese, but be careful with the salt in egg here—Prosciutto is especially salty.

Serves 4.

Veal Birds with Pine Nuts

12 veal scallops
12 slices thin boiled ham
10 sprigs parsley, chopped
½ cup Parmesan cheese, grated
½ cup pine nuts
½ cup seedless raisins
Salt and pepper
3 tablespoons hot olive oil
¾ cup red wine

Place the thin veal scallops (about 5 by 3 inches) between wax paper and pound them thinner. Lay a thin slice of ham on top of each scallop. Mix together the pine nuts, 6 or 7 sprigs of parsley, Parmesan cheese and seedless raisins and put a generous tablespoon of stuffing on each ham slice. Roll up the meat and secure the stuffing with wooden picks or skewers. Salt and pepper the "Birds." Brown them on all sides in olive oil, add red wine and cook them, covered, for about 15 minutes, or until meat is tender. If they're really nice white veal 15 minutes will do. If it's baby beef, cook longer—45 minutes to an hour—or until very tender. Arrange the "Birds" on a heated platter, cover with the sauce, and garnish with parsley.

Serves 6.

Veal Birds with Water Chestnuts

1½ pounds veal, sliced very thin
Salt, pepper, flour
Filling:
4 slices bacon, diced
⅓ cup chopped celery
⅓ cup chopped onion
4 tablespoons chopped parsley

½ cup coarsely chopped water
  chestnuts
½ teaspoon marjoram
2 cups fresh dry bread crumbs
1 cup chicken stock or broth
1 cup good dry red wine

Place thin slice of veal on wax paper, sprinkle with salt, pepper, and a little flour. Cover with another piece of wax paper and pound with flat side of mallet until it is thinner.

Fry bacon crisp; drain. In bacon drippings lightly fry onion, celery, parsley. Add bread crumbs, water chestnuts, marjoram and crisp bacon. Moisten with ½ cup chicken stock. Put a tablespoon of filling on each veal slice. Roll up tightly and fasten with picks or skewers or tie with string. Brown in oil on all sides. Place in casserole or shallow baking dish with a cover. Deglaze pan in which rolls were browned with remaining soup stock and red wine. Pour over birds. Cover, and bake in 350° oven for 45 minutes. If you're lucky enough to have real white veal in your area, less cooking time will be better—if not, or if it's baby beef, you may have to cook longer or until tender—45 minutes to an hour. Bake uncovered the last 15 minutes.

If sauce is not thick enough, remove birds and place casserole on top of stove. Let sauce come to a boil, then lower heat and let simmer until reduced somewhat or add a couple of tablespoons of that Brown Sauce on page 66. Stir over medium heat until thickened. Taste for seasoning. Replace veal birds in the sauce and serve right in your baking dish. If you're not fond of your baking dish, place birds on a warm platter and pour sauce over all.

Serves 4.

Crown Roast of Lamb with Barley Pilaff

1 12-rib crown roast of lamb
Salt

Black pepper, freshly ground

Barley Pilaff

¼ cup butter
⅓ cup shallots or onions,
   chopped (be generous)
1½ cups pearl barley

3 cups light beef bouillon
½ teaspoon black pepper,
   freshly ground
¼ cup parsley, chopped

Melt the butter in a heavy saucepan and gently sauté the shallots. Add the barley and the broth heated to the boiling point. Grind the black pepper into the pot. Stir well, cover, and bring to a boil. Lower the heat so the broth just simmers and cook for 50 minutes to 1 hour, or until the barley is tender to taste and the liquid is absorbed. Add water if the broth cooks away too fast. Taste the pilaff and add salt and more pepper, if necessary. If the broth is well seasoned, salt may not be needed. Toss with chopped parsley and a little extra butter. Use to fill rack of lamb or to serve with other meats.

Have the butcher prepare the crown roast, made from rib chops that have been trimmed of all fat, so the bones look like Frenched lamb chops. Cover the bone tips with foil to prevent charring. Preheat the oven to very hot (450°). Place the meat in roasting pans, season with salt and pepper, and roast for 15 minutes. Lower the heat to medium (350°) and continue roasting for 45 minutes for rare lamb, up to 1 hour or more for well done, depending on the size of the chops. The usual portion is 2 ribs per person. When the meat is done, place the roast on a platter and fill the center with barley pilaff. Place ruffled paper frills on the bone tips and serve immediately.

Serves 6.

Rack of Lamb

4 pound rack of lamb   Salt and pepper to taste
   (2 ribs per person)   1 clove garlic, crushed

Have the butcher make slight incisions between the ribs. Preheat oven to 400°. Protect the ends of the bones by covering with aluminum foil. Rub lamb generously with salt and pepper and crushed garlic. Insert meat thermometer in fleshy part, away from bone or fat. Place lamb, fat side up, on rack in shallow roasting pan and roast uncovered for 45 minutes or until meat thermometer reads 175° for medium or 180° for well-done lamb. Replace foil tips with paper frills.
    Serves 4 to 6.

Lamb Shanks with White Beans

Call your butcher ahead of time to order the lamb shanks—he doesn't always have them in the shop.

2½ cups navy beans
6½ cups water
1½ tablespoons salt
8 to 10 lamb shanks
   (at least 1 per person)
4 lamb bones (ask the butcher for
   these 4 extra bones)
2 large onions, coarsely chopped
2 large carrots, coarsely chopped
4 tablespoons oil

2 cups dry white wine or red wine
   (be sure it's dry)
3 cups beef stock or bouillon (not
   consommé), or more as needed
1 bay leaf
1 teaspoon rosemary or thyme
3 tablespoons tomato paste
3 cloves garlic, whole
Salt and pepper to taste

Soak navy beans in water to cover for 2 hours. Drain. Bring 6½ cups water to a boil, add drained beans and bring quickly to a boil again. Boil for exactly 2 minutes. Remove from heat, set aside, and let them sit for 1 hour. Return to heat, add salt and simmer for 1 hour. Remove from heat and set aside. The beans will finish their cooking with the lamb shanks.

In a large Dutch oven or roasting pan, brown the lamb shanks and bones in oil. Remove shanks and bones to a platter. Add the onions and carrots and sauté until brown. Remove the vegetables to the same platter with the meat. Skim off excess remaining oil. Add the wine to the roaster or Dutch oven and scrape loose all the goodies left from browning meat and vegetables. Bring wine to a boil and reduce by half.

Meanwhile, season lamb with salt and pepper and place fat side up in the Dutch oven or roaster, surrounded by the vegetables. Add beef or brown stock (page 66) or bouillon—you need plenty of sauce with this one. Add the bay leaf, rosemary or thyme, tomato paste and garlic. Bring to a simmer on top of the stove. Lay aluminum foil on top of roaster or Dutch oven and then place cover over that. Place in the lower half of a preheated 300° oven. Turn and baste the meat every half hour. It should take about 2½ to 3 hours for the shanks to cook and be tender and juicy.

Half an hour before the meat is done, remove lamb, vegetables and garlic from the Dutch oven or roaster. Strain and skim the grease from the cooking stock and correct seasonings. Return stock and lamb only to Dutch oven or roaster and add beans. Return pot to stove and bring to a simmer over medium heat. Cover roaster or Dutch oven and return to oven and cook until the meat is fork tender. This should take about 30 minutes. Transfer lamb to a hot platter, surrounded by the beans. Skim grease from the cooking stock or sauce. Pour a little of the sauce over lamb and beans and pour remaining sauce into a hot sauceboat and serve as an accompaniment with the lamb and beans.

You can do all the braising of the meat and the cooking of the beans in the morning and then, 1 hour before serving time, reheat on top of stove. Add beans and bake in a preheated 350° oven for about 30 minutes more.

Serves 8.

Indonesian Satay—A Shish Kebab

Imagine those Indonesian kids. All these years they have been having peanut butter with their Satay instead of jelly.

❡

1½ pounds leg of lamb, trimmed of fat and gristle and cut into 1-inch cubes
½ cup shoyu or soy sauce mixed with 1 teaspoon dark molasses
1 teaspoon red pepper flakes
¾ cup hot water
⅓ cup chunk style peanut butter
½ cup peanuts, toasted in oven crisply and chopped or ground
1 clove garlic, finely chopped
Juice of a lemon
½ cup tomato sauce (4 ounces)
¼ cup soup stock or water
1 teaspoon Tabasco sauce

Mix all ingredients except lamb in a saucepan. Bring to a boil and stir until fairly smooth. Cool to room temperature. Pour half the sauce over lamb cubes. Mix well and let stand a couple of hours. To other half of marinade add the tomato sauce, the soup stock or water, and the Tabasco. When lamb is ready to cook, add its marinade to the sauce, bring to a boil and use for basting and as a dip when serving.

Skewer the marinated lamb and broil over charcoal if possible. If not, then broil under broiler but not too close to the flame.

Serves 4 to 6.

Lamb Shish Kebab

1 4- to 5-pound leg of lamb, trimmed of fat and gristle, and cut into even 1-inch cubes
½ cup olive oil
1 teaspoon oregano
2 bay leaves
2 tablespoons Worcestershire sauce
Juice of 2 lemons
1 cup red wine
Salt and pepper
2 cloves garlic, finely chopped
Mushroom caps
2 green peppers (cut them in quarters, then halve the quarters)
2 medium onions, cut in wedges
3 large firm tomatoes, cut in wedges
Eggplant, cut in cubes (if you like)

Marinate lamb 4 or 5 hours or over night, if possible, in a mixture of the olive oil, oregano, bay leaves, Worcestershire sauce, lemon juice, red wine, salt, pepper and garlic in the refrigerator in a shallow baking dish. The last couple of hours it is marinating, add green pepper and onion wedges, and just before you're ready to cook it, add tomato wedges and eggplant cubes. Turn meat and vegetables in marinade from time to time.

String the cubes of meat on skewers, alternating with vegetables. Broil over charcoal, basting occasionally with the marinade, or under broiler for quick cooking — I'd say about 20 minutes. Heat marinade, strain, and serve as a dip for the skewered lamb.

Serve this with crusty French sour dough, rice pilaff or plain steamed rice, and a spinach salad. None of it's fattening except the rice and rolls and the bacon in the salad!

Serves 8.

Baked Stuffed Pork Chops

4 double-rib pork chops
¾ of a 16-ounce can of whole
    kernel corn, drained
1 cup bread crumbs
3 stalks celery, finely chopped
½ green pepper, finely chopped
4 thin slices of onion

4 green pepper rings, thinly sliced
Salt and pepper
Flour
Butter
Juice from a 16-ounce can of
    tomatoes

Have the butcher cut pockets in the pork chops. Preheat the oven to 300°. Sauté the chopped green pepper and celery in butter in a skillet until slightly soft. Add bread crumbs, corn, salt and pepper to taste. Mix well. Stuff the chops with the mixture. Sprinkle chops lightly with additional salt, pepper and flour, and brown on both sides in butter. Arrange the chops in a baking pan or ovenproof casserole. Garnish each chop with a slice of onion and a green pepper ring. Cover with juice from tomatoes. Bake, covered, for an hour and fifteen minutes. Remove cover and bake until brown and tender, about 15 minutes. Serve with Fresh Applesauce (next page).

Serves 4.

Fresh Applesauce

Cut into quarters 12 large unpeeled tart apples. Put the apples in a saucepan and cook, covered, for about 20 to 30 minutes, or until they are soft. You can sprinkle a little water in the pan, but if you cook the apples over low heat slowly you won't need to add water. Force the fruit through a sieve or a food mill and discard the skins. Some people add cinnamon, sugar and lemon juice to theirs, but I serve mine absolutely pure.

Makes about 3 cups.

Barbecued Spareribs

I've barbecued spareribs over hickory if I could get it—coals if I couldn't—snug and smug in my little world of purists who knew the old way was the only way. These are not Tennessee, Texas, Chinese, or Polynesian barbecued—and don't tell anybody from down home— they wouldn't believe you anyway—these are better.

❧

4 pounds spareribs	2 tablespoons catsup
5 tablespoons sugar	1 teaspoon salt
3 tablespoons honey	1 cup hot chicken broth or bouillon
3 tablespoons soya sauce	

Mix the ingredients and soak the ribs in this mixture for 2 hours. Then bake in oven at 300° for 2 or 3 hours. Baste every now and then with the sauce.

If the ribs are fatty, drop them in boiling water for about 5 minutes before marinating. Then proceed as directed above.

Serves 6.

Barbecued Ham or Pork

I use a pork loin or a fresh uncooked ham for this. First season your loin or ham very well. If you can cook it over hickory or charcoal—all the better. I have one of those outdoor barbecue ovens with an air-tight lid, and I cook it over a very low charcoal fire for many hours so that it cooks through thoroughly and I baste it with the sauce fre-quently. After the first half hour of cooking and turning, I apply the sauce. If you don't have one of those outdoor barbecues, this will work beautifully in your oven. Simply preheat oven to 400°. Season your meat well. Place meat in oven and reduce oven temperature to 375°. Cook for 30 to 45 minutes. Then reduce oven temperature to 300°. Brush with sauce and bake until done, allowing about 35 to 45 minutes per pound, basting frequently with the sauce. I suggest you use a meat thermometer to be sure your pork or ham is well done (185°).

I serve this on hamburger buns with two kinds of barbecue sauce —one very hot and one mild. You can make your sauce hotter by adding a few more red chili pepper pods.

Please don't use bottled hickory smoke sauce on { *my* / *your* } *bar-becued ham or pork.*

❀

Barbecue Sauce

2 onions, quartered	4 cans tomato sauce
8 cloves garlic, halved	10 or 12 little red chili peppers
2½ ounces chili powder	Salt to taste
½ pint oil	1 tablespoon paprika
1¼ cups white vinegar	2 heaping teaspoons plain mustard
½ bottle tomato catsup	Lots of black pepper

Combine the above ingredients. Cook for 1 hour or 2 if you can and have the time. This makes 2 quarts of sauce. It keeps for ages in the refrigerator.

Audrey Wilder's Smoked Pork Loin and Sauerkraut

Billy Wilder is a brilliant director and a gentleman who is an asset beyond price at a dinner party. The men feel the same way about his wife Audrey, a stunningly beautiful woman who does many things well—she designs and makes her own clothes, does her own cooking, and waits for that strategic moment after everybody has sung his little heart out around the piano to come on in a smoky, sultry singing style to top us all! I've thought of organizing the pros to make Audrey go on first and warm them up for us—but I didn't go through with it because she gave me this simple and great recipe one evening not too long ago.

1 smoked pork loin
4 slices bacon, diced
3½ cups canned sauerkraut,
   not drained

2 apples, cored and sliced
Caraway seeds

Sauté bacon in a large, heavy Dutch oven until a little of the fat is fried out. Add sauerkraut, apples, caraway seeds and a little water. Cook for about 45 minutes. Add pork loin and cook just long enough to heat through. I'd say about 15 minutes more.
    Serves 6.

Sausage and Peppers

Frank Sinatra once gave me a cooking lesson as he drove me to the Palm Springs Airport. The subject: Frank's recipe for sausage and peppers.

When I reached my own digs that evening, I couldn't wait to try it out on my own front burner. It was nice but something was missing. I called and lodged my complaint. Then he remembered that little something he had left out—¾ to 1 cup of red wine.

The wine helps a lot. But so did a cooking lesson at 70 miles per hour.

❦

1 lb. hot Italian sausages	3 tablespoons olive oil
3 green peppers	Salt and pepper (optional)
¾ cup red wine	

Remove stems and seeds from peppers and cut into large chunks. In an ovenproof baking dish that can be used on the top of the stove, sauté green peppers in oil until they begin to soften. Sprinkle with a little salt. Lift the green peppers out of the dish and set aside. Brown the sausages in the same baking dish. When browned, add ¾ cup red wine. Cover the pan with foil and bake the sausages in wine in a 350° oven for 40 minutes. (Ovens vary, so cook until the sausage is no longer pink.) Uncover and add the sautéed green peppers. Bake for an additional 30 minutes and serve in same baking dish.

Serves 4.

Fish and Shellfish

Cioppino

I never really had much seafood as a child. Nashville is not exactly New Orleans, nor is fried catfish exactly Shrimp de Jonghe, but once I got a taste of seafood I could hardly get enough. Try the Deviled Crab or Jambalaya or Shrimps de Jonghe or Cioppino—Try them all!

The first Cioppino I ever tasted was the best—and I had it in Hawaii of all places. I've had it many times with many variations since. Here's the one that comes closest to that first never-forgotten experience with Bouillabaisse Italian style—which originated, they tell me, in San Pedro, California.

I can't seem to find a native-born Italian who ever cooked Cioppino, but you'll love it.

2 tablespoons cooking oil
¼ cup butter
2 medium large onions,
    finely chopped
1 leek
2 to 4 cloves garlic (depending on
    your taste), finely chopped
2 green peppers, sliced in
    thin strips
2 16-ounce cans tomatoes

2 or 3 fresh peppercorns
Salt and pepper to taste
½ cup white wine
1 cup clam juice
1 pound of any one or a combination of rock cod, red snapper and/or sea bass (whatever is fresh and available), cut up in little larger than bite-sized pieces*

*You may use any or all of the shellfish. Just make sure you have a big enough pot! The clam and oyster shells should be scrubbed in cold water before placing in the pot.

2 8-ounce cans tomato sauce
1 bay leaf
Pinch of oregano
Pinch of thyme
Pinch of basil
¼ to ½ teaspoon red pepper
  flakes or dash of cayenne
  pepper

½ pound scallops
1 dozen oysters in shells, cleaned
1 dozen clams in shells, cleaned
1 pound uncooked shrimp,
  shelled and deveined
½ pound lobster tails,
  cooked in shell

Sauté onions, leek and garlic in oil and butter in a heavy skillet until lightly browned. Add green peppers and sauté until peppers are soft and onions a golden brown. Transfer all to a large pot or kettle.

Add tomatoes and tomato sauce and, if you have bits of fresh tomatoes left over in your refrigerator, these may also be added. Add salt and pepper and the oregano, thyme, basil, peppercorns, red pepper flakes or cayenne pepper. Let cook slowly for a couple of hours over low heat, stirring occasionally to make sure it isn't burning on the bottom. Taste for seasoning.

Then add white wine and clam juice. Let simmer about 10 minutes more. Twenty minutes before serving, add the red snapper, rock cod and sea bass and simmer about 5 minutes more. Stir lightly now and then during cooking so as not to break up the fish. Then add the scallops and shrimps and simmer about 8 minutes more. About 7 minutes before serving, add the cooked lobster tails and simmer. About 5 minutes before serving, add the oysters and clams. When clam shells start to open, the Cioppino is ready to be served immediately. You can bring the pot it was cooked in right to the table and dish it out into large soup bowls.

With the Cioppino serve a very crusty French sour dough bread. Heat the bread in foil, and then open the foil a few minutes prior to removing from oven so that the crust gets very crisp. All you need with this dish is a light, crisp, green salad and a good Brie cheese.

How many will it serve? Well — maybe the Yugoslavian National Army. Invite at least 10 people — you'll have some left over for you the next day.

Juachinango in Mexico...
Thai Fish in Thailand ... and
Red Snapper here

No one's going to get fat with this one, but they'll feel well fed.

❧

Red snapper filets   Lime juice
Salt and pepper   Butter

Brush a little oil or butter or margarine over red snapper filets. Salt and pepper generously. Broil quickly on each side over charcoal or under a very hot broiler.

Sprinkle generously with lime juice if you have it, lemon if you haven't—but lime is nicer. Pour a little melted butter over the filets before serving and give them another squeeze of lime juice. Then sprinkle with finely chopped parsley. Garnish with limes cut in halves or lemons cut in quarters.

Crab Cakes

1 pound fresh or frozen king crab meat, cut in chunks
¼ cup butter or margarine
¼ cup onions or shallots, minced
3 eggs, beaten
¼ teaspoon salt
2 tablespoons Dijon mustard
¼ teaspoon cayenne pepper

1½ cups bread crumbs, packed lightly into cup (I use thickly sliced egg bread, toasted and torn into small pieces—better than dry fine ordinary bread or toast crumbs)
¼ cup parsley, minced
Oil and butter

Melt butter in a skillet. Sauté onions until transparent but not brown. Add crab meat, bread crumbs and parsley. Then add eggs beaten with mustard, salt and cayenne. Stir lightly. Remove from skillet; spread in baking dish. Chill for at least 1 hour in refrigerator.

Shape into 12 flat thin cakes. Coat first with an egg beaten with 2 tablespoons water, then with fine bread crumbs. Brown on both sides in butter and a little oil until crisp on edges. Serve immediately.

Serves 6.

Stuffed Deviled Crab in Shells

4 cups fresh cooked or canned
   crab meat (be sure to pick out
   membranes and bits of shell
   carefully)
1 teaspoon dry mustard
1 green pepper, finely chopped
1 pimento, finely cut
1 cup milk
3 thick slices white bread, crusts
   removed and cut in large cubes

¼ pound butter
3 tablespoons parsley, chopped
1½ tablespoons onion, grated
¾ teaspoon salt (to taste)
Dash of pepper
Dash of Tabasco sauce
3 tablespoons Worcestershire
   sauce
Bread crumbs

In a heavy pot, melt butter. Add all ingredients except crab meat. Cook 10 minutes, stirring constantly. Add crab meat. Stir carefully to blend but not to break up crab meat too badly. Cook 5 minutes, let cool, and pile high in crab shells or baking shells. Sprinkle bread crumbs over top and heat through in hot (400°) oven until slightly browned on top.

Serves 6.

Creole Jambalaya

2 tablespoons butter
1 tablespoon oil
2 onions, chopped
1 clove garlic, chopped
1 slice ham, cubed
    (approximately ½ cup)
3 tomatoes, chopped
½ cup tomato juice or 1 8-ounce
    can tomato sauce
Salt and pepper
Pinch of thyme
Dash of chili pepper
1 bay leaf

4 cups chicken broth
1 cup rice
1 cup raw shrimp, cleaned
1 cup frozen or cooked lobster
    tails, cut in bite-sized pieces
1 cup crab meat (optional)
1⅓ cups cooked chicken, diced
2 Italian sausages, cut in slices and
    fried until well done
    (optional, but gives a nice
    flavor)
4 ounces sherry

In a large pot, sauté garlic and onions in butter and oil. Add ham. When onions are brown and ham is slightly browned, add tomatoes and tomato juice or tomato sauce. Add bay leaf and season generously with salt, pepper, thyme and chili pepper. Simmer for 10 minutes. Then add chicken broth. When mixture starts boiling, add rice. After the rice has cooked for about 15 minutes, add sausages and whatever shellfish is available, such as uncooked, shelled, deveined shrimp and chunks of frozen lobster tail. Add chicken and then add crab meat at the last minute. Stir frequently until rice is tender. Add a wine glass of sherry. Cook 5 minutes longer and serve with crusty warmed French sour dough bread, Brie cheese and a light, lovely salad.

    Serves 8 to 10.

Shrimps de Jonghe

2 quarts water
2 stalks celery, tops and all
2 carrots, sliced
2 small onions, diced

2 pounds of shrimp, shelled
    and deveined
1 large clove garlic
¾ cup butter

Juice of one lemon
2 teaspoons salt
1 teaspoon black pepper,
   freshly ground
1 sprig of parsley
1 bay leaf

1 teaspoon salt
Pinch of tarragon
Pinch of marjoram
1 cup fine bread crumbs
½ cup dry sherry
Parsley, chopped

In a large saucepan bring two quarts of water to a boil, add celery, carrots, onions, lemon juice, salt, black pepper, sprig of parsley and bay leaf. Simmer for 15 minutes. Add the shrimp and simmer, uncovered, until pink, 2 to 5 minutes. You can either drain or leave the shrimp in the broth until assembling dish.

In a mixing bowl, mash garlic with back of spoon until almost a paste. Add the butter, softened to room temperature, the salt, tarragon and marjoram. Cream them together until well blended; then add bread crumbs and sherry. Blend well. In a large buttered baking dish, place alternate layers of the shrimp and bread crumb mixture, sprinkling chopped parsley over the top of each layer. Bake in a 400° oven for 20 to 25 minutes and serve immediately.

Serves 6.

Goujonnettes of Sole with Tartar Sauce

6 filets of sole, cut into diagonal
   strips about ½-inch wide
1 cup milk
1 egg yolk

Pinch of salt and pepper
3 cups fine fresh bread crumbs
Mustard or tartar sauce

In a shallow dish mix together milk, egg yolk and salt and pepper. Put the strips of fish in the milk mixture and let them stand for several minutes. Lift out the fish strips and coat them completely with bread crumbs. Fry them in hot deep fat (370°) and drain them on paper towels. Serve the fish strips with fried parsley and mustard or tartar sauce.

Serves 4.

Pauline's Seafood Crêpes

30 crêpes

3 (6½-ounce) cans crab meat,
    with membranes removed

or

2 (6½-ounce) cans crab meat,
    with membranes removed and
    ½ pound cooked shrimp,
    finely chopped

1 cup dry white wine

2 teaspoons shallots, chopped

2 tablespoons butter

3 tablespoons flour

3 (½ pint) cartons whipping cream

2 teaspoons Dijon mustard

2 teaspoons Worcestershire sauce

Salt

A few drops of lemon juice or
    juice from ½ lemon

Cayenne pepper

Cook wine and shallots in a saucepan until wine is reduced by half. Meanwhile, melt butter in a large saucepan and add flour. Set on lowest heat. Stir, but do not allow to brown. Add the wine and shallots to the butter-flour mixture, stirring constantly so it won't get lumpy. Add ¾ cup of whipping cream, stirring constantly. Add mustard, Worcestershire sauce, salt, lemon juice and cayenne papper. Taste for seasoning. Divide sauce in half. To ½ the sauce add seafood. Reserve remaining half. Bring seafood sauce to a boil and then cool. Place 2 teaspoons of the sauce on each crêpe, roll up and place side by side in an oblong, shallow, buttered casserole. (Don't crowd the crêpes.) Add remaining whipping cream to reserved sauce. Reheat and pour over crêpes. Sprinkle with Parmesan cheese. Place under broiler — not too close — and watch carefully. Serve immediately.

Crêpes can be made ahead, filled and placed in casserole without sauce in a 325° oven for 10 to 12 minutes to heat through. Cover casserole completely with aluminum foil. When ready to serve, pour sauce over and proceed as above.

Serves 6 to 8.

Crêpes

4 eggs

2 cups milk

¼ teaspoon salt

1 cup flour

Beat eggs well. Add milk, flour and salt, beating all together with a rotary beater until mixture is smooth. Heat a 5-inch iron skillet. Pour in 1 tablespoon of the batter and tip quickly to coat bottom of skillet. Cook over medium heat until small bubbles appear. Shake out of skillet onto a clean dish towel until ready to use or store. When you've made a few and they have cooled, they can be stacked without sticking together to store. Wrap six in aluminum foil and freeze. They thaw out quickly.

I keep a supply of crêpes on hand for this dish (which isn't as complicated as it looks) and for leftover chicken, or with a cheese filling or as a dessert. Thaw them out and heat in foil in a 325° oven for 10 minutes or so. For a quick delicious dessert, brush with butter and serve on a warmed platter with a selection of jams and spoons and your guests can roll their own — a little dab 'll do 'em.

Yields about 30 crêpes.

Shrimp Creole

5 pounds raw shrimp, cleaned, shelled and deveined
4 tablespoons butter plus 2 sticks (½ pound) butter or ½ pound diced bacon
½ pound mushrooms, stems and all, sliced
½ cup Madeira wine or a good dry sherry
3 green peppers, sliced fine
4 onions, chopped fine

2 cloves garlic, chopped fine
4 cups celery, chopped
3 (16-ounce) cans tomatoes
½ cup minced parsley
½ teaspoon black pepper
1 teaspoon each salt, thyme, curry powder
1 red dried pepper, whole or ½ teaspoon cayenne
1 bay leaf

Sauté ¼ cup of the onions in 4 tablespoons butter until soft. Add whole shrimps; toss in butter and cook until they turn pink. Add mushrooms, then Madeira or sherry. Set aside. In another deep, large heavy pot, fry bacon or melt remaining butter. Add onions, green peppers, garlic, celery, parsley and sauté until soft. Add tomatoes, salt, pepper, curry powder, thyme, bay leaf, red pepper or cayenne. When mixture heats through and begins to boil, reduce heat and simmer for 45 minutes.

Fifteen minutes before serving remove pepper pod and bay leaf, add shrimp, onion, mushroom, wine mixture. Cook 15 minutes more. Serve over steamed rice immediately.

Serves 10 to 12.

Chicken, Duckling and Turkey

Deviled Broiled Chicken

2½ pound broiling chicken
Olive oil
Pinch of red pepper flakes, crushed

Salt
3 tablespoons dry, white wine

Split the broiling chicken in half, brush both sides lavishly with olive oil, and sprinkle with a pinch each of red pepper flakes and salt. Cook the pieces 15 to 18 minutes on each side under a preheated broiler — not too close to the heat. They should cook through but not enough to let the surface burn. Cut in sections as desired. Place chicken on a very warm platter. Put the broiling pan, which has caught the juices, over moderate heat and stir in the dry, white wine. Reheat the liquid and allow to boil for 5 or 6 seconds. Pour this sauce over the chicken.
    Serves 2.

Broilers Hungarian

When George and I were first married, we bought a new house in Benedict Canyon. Our mutual agent was a man named Abe Lastfogel, who also handled an incredible star named Fanny Brice, who was not only a great comedienne but also a fabulous cook. She was a fine amateur decorator, as is her daughter, my close friend, Fran Stark.
    Fanny was helping George and me decorate our first home. She was a truly fascinating, awe-inspiring individual, and she gave me this recipe one afternoon when I particularly wanted to impress my new husband with my culinary prowess—which, up until that moment, consisted of fried chicken, pot roast, white cake with chocolate icing, and biscuits. I was a smash, and the marriage lasted 17 years because of that and other little goodies.

I serve this with rice or mashed potatoes. Everybody's on a diet —but you have to have something to soak up the wonderful sauce. To complete the dinner, you need only a light green salad.

❀

6 broiling chickens, cut in half	2½ cups (or more) water
2 onions, finely chopped	Salt and freshly ground pepper
2 cloves garlic, chopped fine	to taste
3 tablespoons tomato paste	Butter, about 3 tablespoons

Brown onions and garlic in butter; remove from butter and save. Brown chickens, adding a little cooking oil to butter if necessary. Turn chickens frequently until golden brown all over. Add water, tomato paste dissolved in a little water, onions, garlic, salt, pepper. Cover tightly and cook very slowly for 2 hours or more, basting every 15 minutes, until chickens are very tender. Serve with steamed rice or mashed potatoes or even noodles. Strain gravy before serving.

Serves 10.

Dr. Krohn's Mother's Chicken

You get recipes under the darnedest situations. This recipe came from my obstetrician's mother. I gained well over the prescribed 15 pounds while carrying my daughter, Melissa—it was closer to 40. The situation wasn't helped any by the fact that every once in a while Dr. Krohn would invite us to one of those marvelous dinners in which his mother urged us to eat a little something—"get a little meat on those bones"—the most welcome words those well-padded bones could have heard at that time. This recipe in itself is not too fattening, but the potato pancakes, the noodle kugel and the mashed potatoes with which she served it did the trick.

She did it Kosher style with salt and cold water and standing overnight in the refrigerator and then pouring boiling water over it and scraping the skin and that sort of thing. You don't really have to do all that. Split your chicken up the back and simply wash it with cold water. Pat dry with a towel and put in a roasting pan.

1 5-pound roasting chicken
2 cups water
Salt
Pepper
Paprika

Ginger root, grated
1 onion, coarsely chopped
2 cloves garlic, coarsely chopped
Chicken fat or butter

Sprinkle with salt, pepper, paprika. Grate a little ginger root over chicken. Add onion and garlic. Rub chicken fat or butter over whole chicken. Add 2 cups water. Cover. Brown in hot (450°) oven. When half-roasted take out chicken and disjoint it. Break out back and other heavy pieces of bone and return to gravy. Cook until tender. When tender, pour off gravy. Dissolve 1 teaspoon of flour in about ½ cup water and pour into gravy and let come to a boil.

Serves 4.

Kleeman's Chicken on Corn Bread

To find where, who or what Kleeman is, please turn to page 154. But first . . . mix your corn bread.

8 chicken breasts
Water
Salt and pepper
Grated ginger

2 stalks celery, tops and all
1 large carrot
4 sprigs parsley
1 whole onion

Cook the chicken breasts in water to cover. Add salt, pepper, grated ginger, celery stalks, carrot, parsley, and onion. Cook until just done. Use the strained broth for your sauce.

Sauce

6 tablespoons onion, minced
1 cup butter
8 tablespoons flour

3 pints chicken broth
½ cup cream or milk
Salt and pepper to taste

Brown minced onion in butter until golden. Add flour. Add chicken broth, cream or milk, salt and pepper. Cook until desired thickness. Slice chicken, place on corn bread, and pour sauce over. Serve extra sauce on the side. You'll need it — it's that good! Be prepared to serve seconds on this one.

Serves 10 to 12.

Corn Bread

1 cup cornmeal	1 teaspoon baking powder
1 cup flour	1 teaspoon salt
½ teaspoon soda	2 eggs
1 cup buttermilk	6 tablespoons shortening

Sift dry ingredients into a mixing bowl. Cut in shortening until well blended. Beat buttermilk and eggs together. Mix with dry ingredients until just blended. Pour into a well-greased oblong baking dish. Bake in a hot oven (400°) for 25 minutes or until done.

Split and serve as directed above. Corn bread should be just baked and very hot when served. It's best that way.

Fried Chicken

2 plump frying chickens, cut into individual pieces	1 teaspoon baking powder
2 cups flour	½ teaspoon dry mustard
Salt and pepper	½ cup butter or margarine
Dash of cayenne	½ cup oil
Monosodium glutamate	Milk

In a paper bag combine the flour, salt and pepper (use plenty of the latter two as chicken must be seasoned through), cayenne, monosodium glutamate, baking powder and dry mustard. Add a few pieces of chicken at a time and shake to coat well. Place oil and butter in a heavy skillet (the big electric one is the best) and heat to 380°. Lift chicken pieces carefully from paper bag and place skin side down in skillet. Cook until dark golden brown on one side. Use tongs to turn without piercing chicken and brown on other side. Cover skillet, turn heat down and cook until done. Remove lid for last 15 minutes for crisp chicken. Remove chicken to warm oven to keep crisp and hot. Drain fat and add a little flour to drippings in pan. Stir until light brown. Add milk slowly until gravy is right consistency. Taste for seasoning. Serve with biscuits.

Before cooking I sometimes soak the chicken for an hour or two in buttermilk to cover. Drain it and pat it dry — and then drop it into the bag with flour and seasonings.

Serves 6.

Baked Fried Chicken

For a large crowd this is so delicate and so simple to prepare, it's sinful—

❦

2 fryers, cut into pieces
1 stick (¼ pound) sweet butter
  (if possible)
2 tablespoons salt
2 tablespoons paprika

Freshly ground black pepper
2 teaspoons cornstarch or flour
2 tablespoons water or broth
½ cup chicken broth or white wine

Preheat oven to 400°. Sprinkle salt, pepper and paprika over chicken pieces and place in a shallow pan in a singe layer. Dot with half the butter. Cover with foil. Place in oven for 20 minutes. Remove foil. Increase oven temperature to 450° and bake 30 minutes. Turn chicken carefully with tongs and dot with the rest of the butter and bake 30 minutes more.

Remove chicken to hot platter. Place roasting pan on top of stove over medium heat. Dissolve 2 teaspoons cornstarch or flour in 2 tablespoons of water or broth. Gradually add to drippings remaining in pan. Then add chicken broth or white wine. Bring to a rolling boil, stirring constantly. Pour over chicken or serve in sauceboat on the side.

This is good cold, too.

Fried Chicken Curry

3 chicken broilers, cut for frying
3 tablespoons butter or margarine
1 tablespoon oil
3 medium onions, finely chopped
2 apples, peeled, cored, and
  coarsely chopped
4 to 6 tablespoons curry powder
1 teaspoon cayenne pepper
1 teaspoon cumin
1 teaspoon coriander

1 teaspoon turmeric
3 ripe bananas, mashed through
  sieve
2 cups clear chicken broth
Lemon juice
Currants
Slivered almonds
1½ cups cream
Salt

Sauté chicken in butter and oil until light brown. Sauté the onions and apples in butter and oil until pale golden brown. Add the curry powder, cayenne, cumin, coriander and turmeric. Cook 5 minutes. Add the chicken, banana and broth. Simmer uncovered 30 to 40 minutes. Add more broth if necessary. Before serving add a squeeze of lemon juice and salt to taste. Remove the chicken to a heated platter. Add the cream, which has been heated, to the sauce remaining in the pan. Pour over the chicken. Sprinkle with currants and almonds. Serve with rice and chutney on the side and moist coconut, if you like.

Serves 10 to 12.

Easy Roast Chicken and Almonds

Excellent

I got this recipe when I was playing in a little Scotch foursome golf tournament up north one summer afternoon. One of the ladies in our foursome had invited everybody in sight to dinner that evening at 7:30. I knew she didn't have any help and it was close to 5:30 when we got to the 18th hole. I figured the evening would be cold cuts and corner delicatessen coleslaw. Well, let me tell you, I've hardly ever had a more delicious surprise.

I serve this with rice or buttered al dente noodles.

❧

2 frying chickens, cut in serving pieces	1 10½-ounce can cream of chicken soup
Salt and pepper	1 10½-ounce can cream of celery soup
1 5½-ounce package slivered almonds	¼ cup dry white wine or vermouth *Water*
1 10½-ounce can cream of mushroom soup	Parmesan cheese

Remove the necks and backbones from the chicken parts and reserve for another use. Season chickens with salt and pepper. Lay in shallow baking dish. Cover with two thirds of the almonds. Mix the 3 cans of soup together with the wine. Pour over the chicken and almonds. Sprinkle Parmesan and remainder of almonds over top. Bake in pre-heated 350° oven for 2 hours.

Serves 6 to 8.

Chicken Fricassee and Dumplings

2 chickens	½ cup celery
Salt	1 bay leaf
Pepper	4 tablespoons chicken fat or butter
Ginger	4 tablespoons flour
Water	2 egg yolks, beaten
½ cup onions	2 tablespoons minced parsley
½ cup carrots	1 can mushrooms

Cut chickens into pieces for serving; sprinkle with salt, pepper and a few grains of ginger. Cover with water and cook slowly for 1 hour. Add the vegetables and bay leaf and continue cooking until chicken is tender. Blend flour and melted chicken fat or butter. Gradually add about 3 cups of the hot chicken broth; season and cook until smooth. Pour onto the beaten yolks; add mushrooms and parsley and pour over chicken.

Serves 6.

Baking Powder Dumplings

2 cups flour	2 tablespoons butter
4 teaspoons baking powder	2 eggs, well beaten
½ teaspoon salt	Milk

Sift flour, baking powder and salt; cut in the butter and add eggs with enough milk to form a heavy drop batter. Drop quickly by the spoonful into chicken broth or boiling water. Cover closely and cook 10 minutes without removing the lid.

Yields 12 to 14 dumplings.

Chicken in Parmesan Cream Sauce

2 2½-pound frying chickens, cut into serving pieces	1 cup + 2 tablespoons light cream
Salt and freshly ground black pepper to taste	¾ cup freshly grated Parmesan cheese
½ cup butter	4 egg yolks, beaten
3 tablespoons flour	¾ cup fresh bread crumbs

Season the chicken with salt and pepper. In a skillet heat half the butter. Add the chicken pieces, skin side down, and cook until browned. Turn the pieces, partly cover the skillet and cook until the chicken is tender, about 30 minutes. Preheat oven to moderate 350°.

In a saucepan, melt the remaining butter, add the flour and stir with a wire whisk until blended. Bring the cream to a boil and add all at once to the butter-flour mixture, stirring vigorously with the whisk until the sauce is thickened and smooth. Stir in 1 tablespoon of the cheese. When it has melted, stir in the egg yolks, lightly beaten with a little of the hot sauce.

Sprinkle the bottom of a flat casserole with ¼ cup of the cheese. Arrange the chicken on the cheese and spoon the sauce over the top. Place the casserole in the oven and bake 5 minutes or until thoroughly heated. Combine the remaining cheese with the bread crumbs, sprinkle over the chicken and broil until golden brown.

Serves 6.

The Benny's Roast Chicken

I dined at Jack and Mary Benny's many evenings and oohed and aahed over this chicken for so long that finally Mrs. King, the Benny's cook, graciously gave it to me. She didn't leave out anything (which is highly irregular for good cooks—see F.S.'s Sausage and Peppers page 79.)

There is a little point of cooking philosophy I should explain here. I give everybody every recipe as completely as I remember it — because I feel that no two people cook alike or use a recipe alike any more than they talk, sing or think or do anything else alike. It has to do with your background, experience, muscles, taste and mood at the time.

❀

Small fryers, less than 2½ lbs. Cut in four pieces. Debone the back. Skin the chickens and wipe off. Dip in melted seasoned butter, then roll in fresh bread crumbs. Cook about 45 minutes in shallow biscuit pan or cooky pan, in hot oven (425°-450°) close to lower burner. Pour butter over and serve quickly. Don't handle chickens. If they need browning, place close to broiler as necessary.

Different Chicken Soup-Stew (A Whole Meal)

We love this around my house.

❧

2 quarts water
1 tablespoon salt
6 slices bacon, chopped, or ¼
    pound salt pork, cut in tiny
    pieces
2 chickens, cut in serving pieces
2 carrots, peeled and sliced
2 onions, cut in half
1 package frozen limas

1 package frozen corn
¼ teaspoon cayenne
Pepper, freshly ground
Couple sprigs of parsley
1 bunch celery, chopped
2 or 3 large potatoes, cut in cubes
1 16-ounce can tomatoes
1 teaspoon sugar
½ pint heavy cream

Boil water with salt. Add chopped salt pork or bacon, 2 cut-up chickens, carrots, onions, limas and corn. Add cayenne, black pepper (generously), couple sprigs of parsley. Cover tightly, bring to a boil. Skim well, if necessary. Cover again and cook slowly for 2 hours. Stir gently but often.

Parboil celery and set it aside. Add potatoes, tomatoes and the sugar to soup mixture. Continue cooking, covered, for 1 more hour. A few minutes before serving, gently pick off the skin from the pieces of chicken where it can be done easily without tearing meat too much — chicken will be very tender by now. Add parboiled celery. Just prior to serving, add the heavy cream. Bring the mixture to a boil. Pour into large heated soup tureen. Serve in soup bowls with crusty French bread.

Serves 6 to 8.

Brown Chicken Pot Pie

Though host and hostess were delightfully trim and apparently could not care less about cooking and gourmet foods, some of the finest meals I ever had were at the home of George Burns and Gracie Allen.

The fact that the meals were consistently good through many cooks and housekeepers, etc., proves that somebody really cared. One memorable dish I have never been able to find a recipe for is this Brown Chicken Pot Pie. After many experiments, I think I have come up with something resembling it. If it's not exactly the same thing, it's good enough to stand on its own.

❀

2 small fryers, cut into individual pieces
1 stick of butter (¼ pound)
4 tablespoons oil
3 cups chicken stock
4 carrots, cut in julienne style
6 stalks of celery, cut crosswise
3 potatoes, cut in cubes

2 medium onions, sliced crosswise
2 cloves of garlic, finely chopped
3 tablespoons brown sauce
(see page 66)
Flour
Salt and pepper to taste
Flaky top pie crust

In a brown paper bag combine the flour, salt and pepper. Add a few chicken pieces at a time and shake the bag to coat lightly. Reserve the remaining flour. In a large Dutch oven, heat the butter and oil and brown the chicken, turning frequently and carefully. Lift out chicken. Sauté the onions and garlic until they are just soft. Add carrots and celery and cook until they are soft, but not too brown. Lift out vegetables with a slotted spoon. Drain all but 4 tablespoons of the butter and oil. Add 2 tablespoons of the seasoned flour to the pan. Stir until it turns brown. Add the brown sauce and chicken stock very slowly, stirring constantly, until it is smooth. Let it simmer for a few minutes. Taste for seasoning. Replace chicken pieces and vegetables. Add potatoes and let the mixture come to a boil. Cover tightly and simmer over low heat for about 1 hour. Let mixture cool and skim off the fat. Remove the meat from the bones of the chicken and transfer the whole mixture to a baking dish. (I use a round Pyrex one.) Cover with aluminum foil and cook in a preheated 350° oven until heated through thoroughly. Slip Bea's Quick Pastry Crust (next page) on the top and bake another 10 minutes.

Before I bake this dish, I make a template the exact shape of the top of the baking dish to be used to cut the pastry dough to the desired shape.

Serves 6.

Bea's Quick Top Crust

1 cup flour
¾ teaspoon salt
½ teaspoon baking powder

3—4 tablespoons cold milk
¼ pound (1 cube) butter (chilled)

Sift flour with salt and baking powder. Cut in cold butter. Sprinkle cold milk over mixture. Form gently into a ball and roll lightly and quickly into desired shape, using template recommended above. Flute edges and bake on cookie tin in preheated 400° oven until lightly browned. Slide on to filling. Brush the top with cream or a beaten egg mixed with a little water so that it will have a glaze on top. Cooking it this way keeps the crust crisp — it can't get soggy. When you have eaten all the crust, reassemble in a smaller baking dish and serve the next day.

Chicken Marengo

George Plimpton may write a cookbook. He told me so after a tennis match one afternoon while we were tasting tested recipes for this cookbook. Specifically, there were three mushroom hors d'oeuvres (in), two quiche (out) and a fudge pie (in). While we were taste testing, he also told me this story about Chicken Marengo.

It seems that Napoleon's premier chef was in a panic because the Emperor wanted his favorite poulet immediately on his arrival at quarters. Only one problem—Monsieur L'Empereur arrived with fifteen more guests than anticipated. No more chickens available. The chef threw in chunks of the local delicacy—lobster. Magnifique! It earned him something like La Croix des Forchettes and the General wanted it at every pit stop thereafter.

My niece, Linda (who is married to the prominent neurosurgeon, Dr. Lyons) gave me this recipe for which I can only bestow all the familial love and gratitude I can muster. After all, I'm not the Emperor.

4 chicken breasts, split
Salt; pepper
Butter
2 tablespoons sherry
2 10-ounce packages lobster tails
½ pound mushrooms
2 tablespoons flour
1½ cups chicken broth

1 tablespoon tomato paste
Bay Leaf, crushed
2 tablespoons fresh chives (or 1 tablespoon frozen or dried)
½ teaspoon salt
⅛ teaspoon pepper
3 ripe tomatoes, quartered

Brown chicken breasts, salt and pepper, in butter. Remove from heat and place in shallow baking dish. Pour sherry over and cover with aluminum foil. Bake till tender (about 30-45 minutes at 350°).

Meanwhile cook lobster tails. Remove meat and cut into bite size pieces. To skillet you browned chickens in add mushrooms (and more butter if necessary). Brown till golden and slightly tender. Remove and save. Now to skillet add flour and enough butter to make 2 tablespoons. Blend in 1½ cups chicken broth and stir till thickened. Add tomato paste, bay leaf, chives, salt and pepper. Simmer 15 minutes. Add mushrooms and lobster to sauce. Add tomatoes and simmer 5 to 8 minutes more (no longer). Pour over chicken breasts and serve.

Serves 6 to 8.

Le Bistro Roast Duckling

I love duckling—but it has to be just right. One of the few places where you can consistently count on your having it "just right" is our little Beverly Hills hangout, The Bistro. Kurt Niklas, owner and managing director, persuaded their fine chef, Joachim Kapp, to part with his secret. It's so simple that really there was no secret at all so I convinced them to share another "secret" with me—their individual Cheese Soufflé on page 118.

Meanwhile, here's the Duckling with my Orange Sauce, which some ducks have been known to fly all the way from Long Island just to be accompanied by.

2 5-pound Long Island
   ducklings
Salt and pepper

3 tablespoons oil or butter, or
   enough to barely cover bottom
   of roasting pan

Melt oil or butter in roasting pan. Wash the ducklings inside and out and dry well. Season with salt and pepper inside and out. Roast uncovered in a preheated 475° oven on each side, except the breast, for 25 minutes each or a total of 1 hour and 15 minutes. Pierce duck from time to time to allow natural grease from duck to run out. When three fourths done, pour excess grease out of roasting pan. Return to oven and finish roasting. Bone and serve.

Serves 6 to 8.

Orange Sauce for Duck

⅔ cup brown sugar, tightly
   packed
⅔ cup granulated sugar
2 tablespoons (scant) cornstarch
2 tablespoons grated orange rind
1½ cups orange juice
½ teaspoon salt

½ cup Cointreau or Grand
   Marnier or any orange-
   flavored liqueur (if you don't
   like the liqueur, use 2 cups
   orange juice)
Skin of ½ orange, cut in very
   thin strips

Combine sugars in saucepan. Add cornstarch, then orange rind, juice, liqueur, salt, orange strips. Simmer until transparent and slightly thickened — about 3 or 4 minutes should do it. Serve it in sauceboat with duckling. The orange sauce is an accompaniment and not a disguise for this duck — so I let people sprinkle a little on top and a little on the side — the duck is crisp and tasty.

Stuffing for Turkey or Chicken

This is one of the oldest recipes I can remember. Everybody and his cousin down South consider it one of his favorites for this is a real Southern corn bread dressing. My mother made it, and so do I.

I don't like it too moist—it has to be a little dry, because the turkey will tend to make it a trifle moist anyhow.

This dressing goes beautifully with chicken, too. Cut the recipe in half—you'll still have some left over. I form cakes out of the left-over dressing. Put the cakes in a shallow baking dish in the oven with the chicken or turkey if you have room, basting them often with the turkey or roast chicken drippings for the last half hour of the time the fowl is cooking. Drizzle a little butter over cakes before serving.

❧

1 green pepper, finely chopped	½ loaf stale bread
2 cups celery, coarsely chopped	1 pan corn bread
2 cups carrots, finely chopped	½ pound butter
2 large onions, finely chopped, or grated, or onion juice	Salt and pepper to taste
	½ cup parsley, chopped

Sauté above ingredients, except breads, in butter. Toast the stale bread and crumble fine. Crumble corn bread when done and add both breads to vegetable mixture. Season to taste with salt and pepper.

I moisten bread and corn bread slightly with stock made from the neck, liver, gizzard and heart of turkey or chicken, plus 1 whole onion, 1 carrot, 1 stalk of celery, 1 whole tomato, 1 whole potato (optional), black pepper and water to cover. Bring to a boil and simmer until giblets are tender. (I use this stock for gravy, too.)

Corn Bread

1 cup cornmeal	½ cup shortening
1 cup flour, sifted	1 cup milk
2 teaspoons baking powder	1 egg
1 teaspoon salt	

Sift dry ingredients into a mixing bowl. Cut in shortening until well blended. Beat milk and egg together. Mix with dry ingredients until just blended. Pour into a well buttered 8-inch square pan. Bake in a hot oven (400°) for 25 minutes or until done.

To use this wonder in your turkey or chicken, season birds inside and out with salt. Fill cavity with dressing but don't pack it too tightly or dressing will be hard and lumpy. Mix melted butter with a little flour and brush turkey or chicken with mixture. Bake breast-down for ⅔ of the time and breast-up just long enough to brown nicely. Keep basting with juices from pan and with melted butter.

Day Later Turkey

Serve your left-over turkey this way.

❧

4 cups left-over turkey breast, sliced, or cut in large chunks	2 cups half-and-half
4 tablespoons butter	Salt and pepper to taste
2 tablespoons flour	4 egg yolks
	¼ cup dry sherry

In a heavy, large saucepan, brown turkey lightly in butter. When lightly browned and coated with butter, sprinkle flour over turkey. Turn gently. Then gradually add 1 cup of half-and-half, stirring gently. Lightly beat the egg yolks, add the second cup of half-and-half, salt, pepper and sherry. Add to turkey mixture gradually. Stir carefully and slowly until it starts to thicken. Taste for seasoning.

Serve over crisp, buttered English muffins that have been toasted on both sides, along with cranberry jelly on the side.

Serves 6.

Turkey Mornay

Or serve your left-over turkey this way.

❧

¾ cup chicken broth	2 egg yolks, slightly beaten
4 tablespoons butter	½ cup Parmesan cheese, grated,
3 tablespoons flour	or Gruyère cheese, finely cut
¾ cup cream	

Heat 3 tablespoons butter in top of double boiler over low heat and stir in flour until blended. Keep heating until mixture bubbles. Remove from heat and gradually stir in the chicken broth and cream. Return to heat and bring rapidly to boiling, stirring constantly; cook 1 to 2 minutes longer. Remove from heat and vigorously stir about 3 tablespoons sauce into the egg yolks. Immediately return mixture to double boiler. Cook over simmering water 3 to 4 minutes. Cool slightly. Add cheese and 1 tablespoon butter at one time and blend in until cheese is melted. Serve hot.

This sauce is lovely with left-over turkey or chicken. Split English muffins with a fork; butter and toast in a preheated 400° oven. Lay warmed slices of leftover turkey or chicken over the crisply toasted muffins and pour generous amount of sauce over all. Sprinkle more grated Parmesan cheese over the top and slip under the broiler to brown just before serving.

Casseroles and One-Dish Meals

◈

Beef-Chicken Tamale Pie

2 plump frying chickens, cut in serving pieces, or 1 large roasting chicken
3 to 4 celery stalks
Salt
6 fresh peppercorns, slightly crushed
Sprigs of parsley
1 whole onion
1 bay leaf
1 tomato
1 cup yellow cornmeal
Jack or Cheddar cheese, grated

2 pounds beef (ground round or ground chuck)
Oil
4 tablespoons chili powder (approximate)
2 16-ounce cans tomatoes
2 16-ounce cans red kidney beans
2 cloves garlic, cut in half
Jalapenos, chopped, or red pepper flakes (optional)
2 cups fresh or frozen cut corn, cooked

Cover chicken with water in a fairly large kettle. Bring to a boil and skim. Add celery, salt, peppercorns, parsley, onion, bay leaf and tomato. Cook until chicken is tender, about 45 minutes to 1 hour. Let chicken cool in broth. When cool, remove meat from bones, set aside, and discard skin and bones.

Strain broth into a heavy saucepan. Take 3 cups of the broth and bring to a boil. Add 1 cup cornmeal to 1 cup of chicken broth and blend until smooth. Stir into boiling chicken broth. Cover and cook over low heat until the mixture thickens to make mush.

Line bottom and sides of an oblong baking dish with mush.

While chicken is cooking, do the following:

Brown beef in a little oil in a heavy Dutch oven. Sprinkle salt and 2 to 3 tablespoons chili powder over the meat. Add canned tomatoes, kidney beans (drained and washed well to remove all traces of the sweet liquid in which the beans are packed), garlic and jalapenos or red pepper flakes. Taste for seasoning. Add 1 tablespoon or more of chili powder, if desired. Let simmer, uncovered, over low heat for a couple of hours or cook in the morning before assembling the dish.

Place a layer of corn over the mush lining; add a layer of cooked chicken, a layer of corn, a layer of the meat mixture. Cover with cheese. Bake 30 minutes in preheated 350° oven. Serve very hot with red pepper flakes on side, if desired.

Serves 10 to 12.

Stuffed Cabbage

I didn't know people were all that hung up about stuffed cabbage until we cooked it one day on the television show. The mail was stupendous—hard on the heels of Frank's spaghetti sauce and Tennessee Lasagna, the all-time toppers. When you taste it you'll see why.

It takes confidence, a touch of class or a paucity of deep serving dishes to serve this right in the Dutch oven—but I did and I do. It's like using chopsticks—somehow it tastes better.

1 pound ground round or sirloin	1 16-ounce can tomatoes
½ cup long grain white rice	1 8-ounce can tomato sauce
Salt and pepper	2 bay leaves
Worcestershire sauce	1 onion, finely chopped
A little prepared mustard	1 scant teaspoon sugar
1 head cabbage	2 tablespoons oil
1 egg	

Cook rice and mix with uncooked meat. Add egg and season well with salt, pepper, Worcestershire and a little prepared mustard. Remove leaves of cabbage whole by cutting out core end. Soak leaves in very hot water until pliable but not limp. Then roll meat mixture in them and seal with toothpicks or tie with string.

Brown onions in oil until golden brown. Add tomatoes, tomato sauce, sugar, salt, pepper and bay leaves. Let sauce simmer for about 10 or 15 minutes until blended. Taste for seasoning.

Place cabbage rolls in Dutch oven or deep casserole with lid. Cover with sauce. Cook covered in 350° oven for 1 hour. You can do all of this in the morning and, 45 minutes before serving, place in preheated 350° oven and cook until cabbage is tender. Serve right in the Dutch oven.

Serves 4 to 6 (figure two cabbage rolls per person).

Cassoulet

I love anything with beans — the first time I had this delectable dish was in one of those "wonderful little restaurants" just outside of Paris. There are a lot of recipes for it — this one is just about perfect.

❧

6 cups small white navy beans
1 bottle dry white wine
2 ducklings or 1 large goose
3 pounds lamb chops, cut in
    1-inch pieces (use bones
    and all)
2 large onions, chopped
2 teaspoons salt

6 cloves garlic, put through press
½ teaspoon thyme
¼ teaspoon pepper
2 8-ounce cans tomato sauce
3 pounds pork chops (more if
    desired)
1½ pounds garlic sausage
    (French, Italian or Polish)

The night before:

Place beans in a large bowl and pour the wine over them. Add water until the beans are covered with liquid. Roast the ducklings or goose and save all the fat after roasting. Remove the meat from the duck and refrigerate.

The following day:

Put the beans and any remaining fluid in large pot. Add enough water so that beans are covered. Simmer for 1½ or 2 hours or until beans are tender. They will absorb most of the liquid while cooking.

Sauté the onions and garlic in the fat from the duck. Add the cut-up lamb pieces and sauté about 10 minutes. Set aside.

Add the onion, garlic, lamb mixture to the beans. Add the salt, thyme, pepper and tomato sauce and mix thoroughly. Add any remaining duck gravy and fat and stir again. Taste for seasoning.

Layer the bean mixture with the duck or goose meat and the sautéed pork chops in a very large casserole or roasting pan that has a tightly fitting cover. Top with slices of garlic sausage. If mixture seems

too dry, add a little white wine. Cover the casserole and bake at 350°
for 45 minutes. Remove the cover and bake an additional 15 minutes.
Serve very hot. Can be frozen.
Serves 14 to 18.

Chicken Tetrazzini

Tried this but no-one liked it very much.

1 large stewing hen	3 tablespoons butter
1 pound thin spaghetti	2 tablespoons flour
2 tablespoons butter	2 cups chicken broth (use broth
1 large onion, chopped	remaining after stewing hen)
1 large green pepper, chopped	1 cup heavy cream (heat)
½ pound fresh mushrooms,	2 tablespoons sherry
chopped	½ pound (2 cups) Parmesan cheese
4 ounce can pimentos, chopped	Salt and pepper to taste

Stew hen with any seasoning you prefer (onion, celery, salt and pepper)
until tender. Reserve broth. Skin and bone hen and cut in small pieces.
Cook spaghetti in broth, adding more water if necessary, until just
barely tender. Drain.

Melt 3 tablespoons butter in saucepan and stir in flour. Gradually
add chicken stock and cook over low heat stirring constantly until
sauce comes to boil. Add cream and cook another minute. Add sherry
and about three-quarters of the Parmesan cheese. Add sautéed onion
and green pepper mixture and stir until cheese has melted. Remove
from heat.

Divide this sauce in half. Mix one half with diced chicken and the
other with spaghetti. Put spaghetti in a large casserole. Make a large
hole in the center and pour in chicken mixture. Sprinkle with remaining
cheese. Bake uncovered for 30 minutes at 375° or until light brown.
Serves 10 to 12.

Mother's Chili Con Carne

There is hardly a soul west of the Atlantic seaboard imbued with the good old American cookout spirit who doesn't have his or her own superb recipe for Mexican chili. (No self-respecting Mexican citizen I ever met has ever heard of any of these concoctions.) I am no exception, but I tell you with all due modesty that mine really is the best. This is as close as I remember my mother's recipe, with a little incidental variation learned from other California transplants

❦

Oil
2 pounds ground round steak
2 16-ounce cans tomatoes
3 16-ounce cans red kidney beans
6 cayenne pepper pods
3 whole dried red peppers (or less)

4 jalapenos, seeded and chopped
2 teaspoons cumin powder
3 tablespoons chili powder, or to
taste
2 cloves garlic, cut in halves
Salt and pepper

Drain and wash kidney beans to get rid of all traces of the sweet flavored liquid in which they are packed. If you want, you may use dried red kidney beans or pinto beans which you have soaked over night and cooked according to the directions on the package. I personally prefer the canned variety.

Brown meat well in light oil (peanut, if possible), season generously with salt, chili powder, and dried peppers. Add tomatoes; let simmer for a little while. Season again with salt and chili powder. Add pepper pods, garlic, jalapenos (these are canned Mexican semi-hot chili peppers) and cumin. Add beans and season again if necessary. Cook slowly for 4 hours. It can be prepared in shorter time, but full flavor comes from longer cooking. Garlic and pepper pods can be removed before serving.

Serves 10.

Baked Stuffed Eggplant

Eggplant is like Pumpkin Soup or Stuffed Cabbage. Some people simply will not try it. This is a delicious but sneaky way to prove how wrong they are. You can tell them it's Stuffed Purple Bananas.

❦

1 good-sized eggplant
½ pound ground beef
4 tablespoons green pepper, chopped
2 small onions, finely chopped
2 cloves garlic, finely chopped
2 tablespoons pimento, chopped

2 tablespoons parsley, chopped
½ teaspoon fines herbes
¼ cup dry white wine
Salt and pepper to taste
2 eggs
Parmesan cheese

Cut eggplant in half. Hollow out thoroughly, but save eggplant shell. Chop up the eggplant meat. In a skillet heat 1 tablespoon of oil and 2 tablespoons of butter. Brown the onion and garlic until light golden brown. Add the green pepper and cook until it softens. Add ground beef and brown until there is no red showing. Add salt, pepper and fines herbes. Add chopped eggplant meat to skillet. Let cook until eggplant meat is soft and mixture begins to blend. Then add pimento and parsley. Simmer for about 5 minutes. Add the wine and cook over a low flame for about 25 minutes. Pile the mixture into the hollowed out eggplant shell which you have softened a little by sautéing in oil in another skillet and have seasoned with salt and pepper.

Make two indentations in the center of the eggplant mixture and break an egg into each hollow. Sprinkle with Parmesan cheese and a couple strips of pimento. Place eggplant in a shallow baking dish to which you have added about ½ inch of water. This keeps the eggplant from drying out and softens the shell. Bake in a 350° oven for 25 minutes. Serve piping hot. You can bake this without the eggs and just before serving garnish with two fried or poached eggs with a strip of pimento placed over each egg.

Serves 4.

Moussaka

3 medium-sized eggplants
3 large onions, finely chopped
2 pounds lamb or beef, ground
3 tablespoons tomato paste
½ cup red wine
½ cup parsley, chopped
¼ teaspoon cinnamon
Salt to taste
Black pepper to taste, freshly
  ground

1 cup butter
6 tablespoons flour
1 quart milk
4 eggs, beaten until frothy
Nutmeg
2 cups ricotta cheese or cottage
  cheese
1 cup fine bread crumbs
1 cup Parmesan cheese, freshly
  grated

Peel the eggplants and cut them into slices about ½ inch thick. Brown the slices quickly in 4 tablespoons of the butter. Set aside.

Heat 4 tablespoons of butter in the same skillet and cook the onions until they are brown. Add the ground meat and cook 10 minutes. Combine the tomato paste with the wine, parsley, cinnamon, salt and pepper. Stir this mixture into the meat and simmer over low heat, stirring frequently, until all the liquid has been absorbed. Remove the mixture from the fire.

Preheat the oven to moderate (375°).

Make a white sauce by melting 8 tablespoons of butter and blending in the flour, stirring with a wire whisk. Meanwhile, bring the milk to a boil and add it gradually to the butter-flour mixture, stirring constantly. When the mixture is thickened and smooth, remove it from the heat. Cool slightly and stir in the beaten eggs, nutmeg and ricotta cheese.

Grease an 11 x 16-inch pan and sprinkle the bottom lightly with bread crumbs. Arrange alternate layers of eggplant and meat sauce in the pan, sprinkling each layer with Parmesan cheese and bread crumbs. Pour the ricotta cheese sauce over the top and bake 1 hour, or until top is golden. Remove from the oven and let it cool a little before serving. Cut into squares and serve.

The flavor of this dish improves on standing 1 day. Reheat before serving.

Serves 8 to 10.

Black-Eyed Peas

Black-Eyed Peas eaten on New Year's Eve and New Year's Day bring good luck for the whole following year. I don't know the sage who coined this lovely prognostication, but I never take a chance on challenging him. I want all the good luck I can get—starting with the first day of every New Year—so I carry that little pot of Black-Eyed Peas with me to some of the finest New Year's Eve parties imaginable—black tie or otherwise. They are easy to prepare, delicious, fattening and intriguing. Because of the legend involved, I've created more than a few "believers" in our never-never land of tinsel, talent and lucky breaks.

❧

1 2-pound package dried
    black-eyed peas
1 ham hock with ham bone, or
    left-over ham bone, or ½
    pound lean bacon

2 medium onions, whole
2 cloves garlic, whole
2 red pepper pods, whole
Salt to taste

In a large kettle or pot, soak peas over night in water to cover, or follow directions for cooking on package. (I find the peas are a little less mushy and a little less likely to fall apart if you do it the old way—soaking over night.) Drain the next morning. Add cold water to cover. Then add onions, garlic, red pepper pods, ham and salt to taste. Cover and bring to a boil. Reduce heat and simmer very gently over low, low heat for at least 2½ hours (or longer if you can). Taste from time to time for seasoning. If the beans begin to get too dry, add more water. (I let mine sit over the lowest possible heat practically all day, partially covered.) Remove the onions, garlic and red pepper pods before serving.
    Serves 10.

Variation: To make Black-Eyed Pea Soup, purée 2 cups of peas and leave 1 cup whole. Add 2 cans of chicken broth. Heat thoroughly. Cut the ham off the ham bone into small chunks. Place on the bottom of each soup bowl. Garnish with grated egg.
    Serves 6.

Piroshki

This is an authentic delicious cold winter's night fried Russian meat pie. George's sister, Mary, taught me how to make it, and I thanked her effusively. Maybe I shouldn't have—everybody gets sore at me when I serve it, because they always overeat.

❦

1 quart milk	½ cup warm water
2 tablespoons sugar	3 sifter-fulls (about) flour, ½ hard
2 tablespoons oil	and ½ soft wheat
⅛ pound butter	1 scant tablespoon salt
2 cakes yeast	2 eggs

Warm milk, salt, sugar, oil and butter together. Dilute yeast cakes in water and add to milk mixture. Then add eggs to milk mixture. Sift flour into it to make dough. Work dough for 15 minutes or so. Cover and wrap towels around and set in a warm place. When risen, press down, cover, and let rise again.

Filling

5 medium large onions,	1 pound beef liver
chopped fine	2 pounds ground round
⅛ pound butter	5 hard-boiled eggs, chopped
3 tablespoons oil	Salt and pepper to taste

Brown onions in butter and oil until golden. Then brown the liver and ground round until juicy. Add the eggs and season to taste.

Take the dough and roll it with your palms into a long cylinder about 2 inches in diameter. Slice off a piece of the roll about 1½ inches thick. On a lightly floured board, place your circle of dough, cut side down. Work outward lightly with your fingertips, stretching dough until it's about 3½ inches in diameter.

Place a teaspoon of the filling in center of circle. Take opposite sides of dough and bring together at top gently over meat filling. Start pressing together, starting at the center top and working on down each side of the little meat pie, until it makes a completely sealed semicircle. Let the piroshkis sit in a warm place until you're ready to fry them in deep hot fat. They'll rise again, and when they cook they'll expand even more. They get golden brown—crisp on the outside, juicy on the inside. Serve with a bowl of sour cream for each two people—you dip each bite in sour cream as you go.

Serves 10 to 12.

Harmony McCoy's Soul Food

Harmony McCoy is a hearty gentleman who cooks healthy diet dishes at a fat farm near Los Angeles. When I went to the aforementioned spa to break the weight barrier one time, we were fed 700 to 800 calories a day and even those dishes were delicious. I learned subsequently he never touches the stuff. Why should he? He's already down to 245 pounds from 300 by eating things like this.

❦

10 beef or pork neck bones with meat on (figure on two per person)
2 quarts salted water
1 onion, chopped
3 or 4 dried red chili peppers, crushed
2 pounds canned sauerkraut, drained
½ onion, grated
2 potatoes, boiled
1 cup flour
4 eggs

Put neck bones in a large pot and cover with salted water. Add the chopped onion, chili peppers and cook until fork tender—about 3 hours. Remove neck bones and set aside. Mash potatoes. Add grated onion and then add the unbeaten eggs to the mashed potatoes. Blend thoroughly. Then slowly add flour until batter is the consistency for dropped dumplings. Drop batter quickly by tablespoonfuls into the boiling beef or pork broth. Cook dumplings uncovered. They will settle to bottom of pan; when they rise to the top, cook for 2 minutes longer. Remove dumplings and set aside with meat. Add drained sauerkraut to broth and cook for an additional 30 minutes. Return neck bones and dumplings to broth. Cover and simmer over low heat for 10 minutes.

To assemble, place neck bones on a warm platter or in a large tureen. Place sauerkraut over neck bones, then add dumplings. Pour the broth in which the neck bones and sauerkraut were cooked over all.

Serves 6.

Tennessee Lasagna

My version of lasagna is one of those dishes that is most useful when people unexpectedly drop over and you have to substitute several ingredients to make it stre-ee-etch.

On one occasion I added cheese. On another, more macaroni.

It's an economical dish, and my usual practice is to make two and put one in the freezer. Then whenever guests drop in unexpectedly, as they say in the commercials, I pop the frozen one in the oven.

What's more, Tennessee Lasagna reheats well, and it's good the second day. Reassemble it in a smaller casserole, sprinkle more cheese over the top, add tomato juice if you need it, and reheat slowly and thoroughly.

I've hardly ever had a more accommodating dish.

❦

Cook one 1-pound package of elbow macaroni in salted water until just done.

1 pound of sharp Cheddar cheese, cut in cubes	Parmesan or Cheddar cheese, grated

Sauce

2 pounds ground meat (ground chuck or 1 pound ground chuck and 1 pound hot Italian sausage, if you like)	6-8 whole mushrooms, sliced thin
	4 cups tomatoes (2 16-ounce cans)
	1 8-ounce can tomato sauce
1 small bunch of celery, coarsely cut	Dash of Worcestershire sauce
2 cloves of garlic, chopped fine	Pinch of oregano
1 medium onion, chopped coarsely	1 teaspoon chili powder
1 green pepper, cut in broad strips	Red pepper flakes
	¼ teaspoon cumin

Brown onions and garlic in oil, then add celery and green pepper. Cook until a little soft. Remove from pan. Add ground meat to oil and brown well. After meat is browned, add salt, pepper, chili powder, cumin, Worcestershire sauce, oregano (easy on this), mushrooms, onions, garlic, celery and green pepper. Sprinkle with red pepper flakes. Add tomatoes and tomato sauce. Allow to cook slowly for one hour until sauce blends.

Assemble by putting a layer of macaroni in casserole—dot with butter, add cheese cubes and then a layer of the sauce. Sprinkle with red pepper flakes. Then another layer of macaroni, butter and cheese cubes, etc., finishing with a layer of sauce.

Top with grated Parmesan or Cheddar cheese. Bake in a 350° oven for 30 minutes until cheese is melted inside and dish is thoroughly heated. This can be prepared ahead and reheated 30 minutes before serving. This is good the next day too. Just reassemble what you have left over in a smaller casserole, add a little tomato juice if it seems dry, grate cheese over top and heat through thoroughly.

Serve with crusty French bread.

Serves 10 to 12

Pastel De Choclo Y Maiz
(Chilean Meat and Corn Casserole)

Hugo Samuels is a Chilean gentleman's gentleman, singer, butler, and now chef. He works for some friends of mine. One busy Saturday morning, he dropped something off from them and noticed me slaving away at the advance work on our tennis lunch—the players were due shortly and I couldn't bear to miss a set. He volunteered a Chilean dish for lunch. I accepted. Two hours later he arrived with this steaming casserole and two heavy pot holders in hand. The dish was naturally the success it deserved to be. Hugo wrote it down for me in English. It's an unusual and spicy combination of flavors and textures. Try it—you'll love it!

3 onions
1½ pounds beef, chopped
1 green pepper
2 cloves garlic
2 chicken breasts
2 hard-boiled eggs
1 cup raisins
12 ripe olives, pitted
3 boxes frozen corn
3 tablespoons cornstarch

1 cup milk
Paprika
Salt
Pepper
Bay leaf
Oregano
Cumin seed
Chili powder
Tabasco sauce

Soak raisins in water to cover until plump; then drain well. Cook the chicken breasts until just done in water to which you've added ½ onion, stalk of celery, 2 sprigs of parsley, salt and pepper. Save broth to use for cooking corn.

While the chicken breasts are cooking, finely chop the onions, peppers and garlic. Sauté in olive oil and a tablespoon of butter, and season with paprika, salt, pepper, bay leaf, oregano, cumin seed, chili powder and Tabasco sauce. When this is half-cooked, add the chopped beef. Cook over low heat until meat is completely browned. Add the raisins. After a few minutes add the olives. Let stand for half an hour off the heat, with the cover on.

Cook the corn over medium heat for a few minutes in ½ cup milk and chicken broth, or ½ cup milk and water. Add salt and sugar to taste. Then put the corn and liquids in a blender and purée. Return the mixture to the burner over moderate heat and add the cornstarch which has been dissolved in a little milk. Cook for 5 minutes.

In a baking dish—a shallow oblong casserole makes for easy serving—place a layer of beef-onion mixture, slices of chicken breast, slices of egg, and cover with the corn cream mixture. Sprinkle a little brown sugar over the top. Bake in a 400° oven for 20 minutes; then place under broiler until top is slightly brown.

Serves 8.

Sausage Cornmeal Pie

2 pounds sweet or Italian hot
   sausage, or half and half
1 cup sliced onion
1 clove garlic, crushed
1 16-ounce can of tomatoes
1 8-ounce can of tomato sauce
1 scant teaspoon salt

½ teaspoon oregano
½ teaspoon sugar
¼ teaspoon basil
¼ teaspoon black pepper
1½ cups yellow cornmeal
¾ teaspoon salt
1 cup grated sharp Cheddar cheese

Preheat oven to 375°.

Cut all but three sausages into 1-inch pieces; halve remaining three sausages lengthwise for decorating top.

Brown sausage in a large heavy skillet or Dutch oven. Cook over medium heat until cooked through, turning frequently. Drain on paper towels. Discard all but 1 tablespoon of the fat. Use the remaining fat to sauté onions and garlic until golden brown. Add tomatoes, tomato sauce, salt, oregano, sugar, basil, pepper and sausage pieces to sauce. Turn up heat. When sauce boils, lower heat and simmer uncovered for 25 minutes, stirring occasionally.

In a large saucepan, combine cornmeal with 3 cups water and salt. Bring to a boil, stirring constantly. Boil until thickened. Remove from heat and let cool a few minutes.

Assemble casserole. Use a 2½-quart baking dish. Cover bottom with half of the cornmeal mixture. Add the sausage and tomato mixture, then add half of the cheese and cover all with the rest of the cornmeal, and then the remaining cheese.

Arrange sausage halves on top and bake uncovered in a 375° oven for 30 minutes until heated through.

Serves 6 to 8.

Cheese, Rice, Pasta, Potatoes

◈

Cheese Pit

5 slices bread, buttered and cut
   in cubes
¾ pound sharp, tangy Cheddar
   cheese, coarsely grated
4 eggs, beaten

2 cups milk
1 teaspoon dry mustard
1 teaspoon salt
Dash of cayenne pepper
Dash of Worcestershire sauce

Alternate layers of bread and cheese in a greased casserole. Mix milk, dry mustard, salt, pepper and Worcestershire sauce and add to the eggs. Mix and pour over cheese and bread. Let stand several hours—or better over night. (It can stand even 2 nights in refrigerator.) Bake 1 hour at 350°.

This is similar to cheese soufflé but it does not need to be served immediately and will wait for guests. It is good served with ham or alone as luncheon dish.

Serves 6.

Le Bistro's Cheese Soufflé

1 cup clarified butter (melt butter
   in a saucepan; skim off foam,
   and leave sediment in bottom of
   pan)
1 cup flour
Salt and pepper
Nutmeg

2 pints milk
½ pound sharp Cheddar cheese,
   grated
2 generous cups Parmesan cheese,
   grated
8 egg yolks
15 egg whites, approximately

To clarified butter add flour, salt, pepper and nutmeg, and stir until well blended. Add milk (⅓ cold, ⅔ hot) gradually and stir until thoroughly blended. Add Cheddar cheese, stirring until cheese is melted. Remove from heat. Add egg yolks and half of Parmesan cheese. Remove to a large bowl and top with rest of Parmesan cheese. Let cool. Beat egg whites with a wire whisk, in a copper bowl if you have one, until *almost* stiff. Fold ⅓ of egg whites into mixture in bowl. Beat remaining egg whites until stiff and fold into mixture carefully.

Butter and flour six 9-ounce soufflé dishes. Fill each about ⅔ full. Bake in a preheated 400° oven for 25 to 30 minutes. Serve immediately.
Serves 6.

Pauline's Cheese Soufflé

Pauline, as you can see, makes this with 4 eggs. I add two extra whites. I don't want to press my luck.

❧

4 tablespoons butter	1 cup milk
4 tablespoons flour	1 cup aged sharp Cheddar
1 teaspoon salt	cheese, finely grated
Paprika	4 eggs, separated
Cayenne or Tabasco sauce	

Melt butter in double boiler. Add flour, seasonings, and blend well. Add milk and cook until thick. Add cheese and stir until melted. Cool and add egg yolks, well beaten. Beat egg whites with a wire whisk until stiff but not dry (I beat my eggs in an unlined copper mixing bowl—they seem lighter and fluffier somehow). Stir ¼ cup beaten egg whites into flour-egg-cheese mixture. Then fold in remainder of egg whites, gently and carefully so as not to lose the air you beat into them. There may be some streaks of beaten egg white remaining when you pour mixture into a well-buttered 5-cup soufflé dish. Bake in a preheated 475° oven for 10 minutes, then reduce heat to 400° and bake about 25 minutes longer. Serve at once or sooner.
Serves 4.

Macaroni and Red Wine Meat Sauce

¼ cup oil
1 cup onions, chopped
2 cloves garlic, chopped
1 pound ground round or chuck
   steak
¼ teaspoon dried rosemary,
   oregano and sweet basil
2 teaspoons salt
Pepper, freshly ground

2½ cups canned tomatoes
5 tablespoons tomato paste
1 cup dry red wine
½ teaspoon sugar
1 12-ounce package elbow
   macaroni
1 cup Parmesan cheese, grated
½ cup parsley, chopped

In a large heavy skillet, brown the onions and garlic in hot oil until transparent. Add meat and stir until brown. Season with salt and pepper. Dissolve the tomato paste in wine. Sprinkle herbs over the meat. Add tomatoes, tomato paste-wine mixture, and sugar. Simmer until blended—about 1 hour or more if you have time. Sauce should not be too thick. Add wine, water or tomato juice as needed. Cook macaroni until just done—not too soft. Drain and rinse in hot water. Be sure macaroni is well drained. Place on warm serving dish or casserole. Add hot meat sauce and Parmesan and sprinkle with parsley. Toss gently. Serve with more cheese if you need it.

Serves 6 (or 8 as a side dish).

Pasta Fazool

Well, that's the way it always sounds to me. It's really PASTA E FAGI-OLI. Pasta—macaroni in this case—and white beans. Tony Charmoli's mother cooked this dish the first time I ever tasted it and it's a lulu. Tony created all those marvelous energetic dance routines on our Chevy Shows. I had to dance a lot to counteract the effects of this one.

1 pound white small navy beans
1 stalk celery, chopped
1 clove garlic, finely chopped
1 onion, chopped
5 tablespoons olive oil
Ham bone (with a little meat
    left on)
2 quarts boiling salted water

½ cup pasta (macaroni)
2 tablespoons pesto (½ teaspoon
    basil, small garlic clove, 2
    tablespoons Parmesan cheese,
    2 tablespoons pine nuts
    [optional] and 1 tablespoon
    olive oil mashed together into
    a paste)

Soak the navy beans over night. In a soup pot, sauté the celery, garlic and onion in 2 tablespoons of olive oil until lightly browned. Add the ham bone and the drained beans and pour in boiling salted water. Simmer the soup about 3 hours, then take out the ham bone and about 1½ cups of the beans, choosing those that remain whole.

Cut the meat off the ham bone, dice it. Pass the rest of the soup through a coarse sieve and return to the pot. Add the whole beans and 1 cup of the ham. Bring the soup to a boil, add pasta and the rest of the olive oil and boil the soup gently until the pasta is cooked. Pour the soup in a hot tureen containing the pesto. If the soup is too thick, add a little boiling water or broth. Serve with grated Parmesan cheese for the soup, and with toast immediately following. Then dance a lot.

Serves 8 to 10.

Parmesan Toast

1 loaf French sour dough bread,
    cut into thick slices
1 cube soft butter
1 teaspoon paprika

¾ cup Parmesan cheese, finely
    grated
½ clove garlic, crushed (optional)

In a bowl, mix butter, Parmesan cheese, garlic and paprika. Toast 1 side of the bread. On the untoasted side, spread butter-cheese mixture and place in a preheated 400° to 450° oven until cheese is melted and bread is heated through.

Yields 10 slices.

Frank's Fresh Tomato Sauce for Spaghetti

Frank who? Frank happens to be a friend of mine who sings a little and as you can see from Sausage and Peppers on page 79 cooks a lot. He appeared on my television show and cooked this sauce and talked and sang. Mama Mia, some spicy program!

❧

2 tablespoons olive oil	¼ teaspoon basil
¼ onion, sliced into thin crescent wedges	Pinch of oregano
	Parsley
1 No. 2½ can Italian peeled tomatoes	1 pound spaghetti
	4 cloves garlic
½ teaspoon pepper	Grated Romano cheese
½ teaspoon salt	Hot dried chili peppers

Put 2 tablespoons of salt into a 4-quart pot of water and bring to boil.

In a frying pan heat olive oil; add onion and garlic cloves. Sauté until brown and remove the garlic.

Place the tomatoes in a blender with some of the liquid from the can and mix gently—less than a minute.

Slowly pour the tomatoes into the frying pan. Be very careful because the liquid on the oil has a tendency to explode. Let this simmer for about 15 minutes, after adding seasoning.

When the spaghetti, which has been placed in the boiling water, is done (test by tasting the spaghetti), pour the sauce over. Sprinkle with parsley and serve.

Serve with small side dishes of red pepper flakes and Romano cheese, hot crusty French bread and Italian red wine. Don't forget the red checkered tablecloth.

Serves 4.

Godfrey Cambridge's Spaghetti Alla Carbonara

Godfrey is a very funny man—he also has had a little weight problem from time to time—I trust almost anybody who has these two qualities going for him. Godfrey cooked this dish on my TV show—It's more delicious than it is funny.

1 pound spaghetti or spaghettini
¼ pound butter
¼ cup heavy cream
Black pepper, crushed
Dash of oregano

15 slices bacon, fried crisp and
　crumbled
3 egg yolks, beaten slightly with
　a wire whisk
Parsley, chopped

Cook spaghetti or spaghettini according to directions on package until just done—al dente. Melt butter, add cream, black pepper, oregano and bacon. Simmer, stirring 5 minutes.

Drain spaghetti or spaghettini thoroughly in a large colander. Transfer it to a heated serving bowl and stir in the beaten, raw egg yolks, which will cook on contact with the hot pasta. Stir in the cream-butter sauce and mix thoroughly. Garnish with parsley.

Serves 6 as a side dish.

Spaghettini with Prosciutto and Mushrooms

1 pound spaghettini
¼ pound prosciutto (Italian ham)
　minced, or ½ pound lean
　bacon, diced and cooked
　crisply—drained and kept warm

½ pound mushrooms, sliced
½ cup butter
Parmesan cheese
2 tablespoons cream (optional)

Cook spaghettini according to directions on package until just done al dente. Add a little oil to the water to keep the spaghettini from sticking together. When spaghettini is cooked, drain, rinse thoroughly with cold water and let sit in a colander.

In a large deep skillet, sauté the mushrooms in ¼ cup butter until lightly browned. Add the prosciutto. (If you are using bacon instead of prosciutto, do not add the bacon at this time.) Add the spaghettini to the mushrooms and ham. Sprinkle with Parmesan cheese and ¼ cup more butter and cream, if you like. Toss lightly. (Now, add bacon.) Toss just prior to serving and sprinkle more Parmesan cheese on top. Serve immediately.

Serves 6 as a side dish.

Spaghetti Sauce

6 medium large onions, finely chopped
1 carrot, chopped
4 cloves garlic
2 pounds ground chuck
1 pound ground pork sausage

Salt
Pepper
3 cans tomato sauce
2 cans tomato paste
2 cans water

Finely chop the onions and garlic and brown in oil. Add chopped carrot. Then add ground chuck and ground pork sausage. Cook until well browned. Salt and pepper generously. Add tomato sauce, tomato paste and water. After it has bubbled, season with salt and pepper again, turn flame very low and simmer as long as you can—2 to 3 hours preferably.

Cook spaghetti according to the directions on the package. Cook until just done but *not* soft.

To assemble

Mix a little sauce with your spaghetti—gently. Pour the rest of the sauce over the top. Sprinkle with Parmesan or Romano cheese. A crisp green salad and parmesan toast (page 121) is all you need here.

Serves 6 to 8.

Barley à la Tomato à la Colony Restaurant

This has always been one of my favorite dishes and I discovered it early in my career through a great and dear friend named Manie Sacks, whose favorite restaurant was The Colony in New York. They have so many good dishes on that menu. I took hours trying to decide what I wanted for dinner (I really wanted some of everything). Manie managed it—he ordered for all of us. Each entrée was very special, and we had a little sample of those, but we each had our own full portion of this particular dish because it was his favorite. It became one of mine and I can never seem to get enough of it. When I started doing this cookbook, I asked the owner, Gene Cavallero, for the recipe and he came through.

1 cup barley	½ cup Meat Sauce (see below)
Salt and pepper to taste	Parmesan cheese, grated
½ cup tomato sauce	

Cook barley according to directions on package. Drain and rinse well. Add salt and pepper. Mix tomato and Meat Sauce. Add barley. It should not be too dry so add plenty of sauce. Place in a shallow oven-proof casserole. Sprinkle with grated Parmesan cheese. Place in a preheated 350° oven for about 10 minutes until mixture is heated through. Then place under broiler for a few minutes until cheese is melted and bubbling. Serve immediately.

    Serves 4.

Meat Sauce

1 tablespoon butter or oil	1 tablespoon tomato paste
1 onion, finely chopped	2 cups Brown Sauce (see page 66)
½ pound ground beef	or if you don't have it see
1 clove garlic, crushed	below. But have it, please.
2 tablespoons dry sherry	

Sauté onions in melted butter or oil until lightly browned. Add ground beef and brown until all the red color is gone. Add garlic, sherry and tomato paste and simmer for 20 minutes, stirring occasionally. Add the Brown Sauce and simmer for an additional 30 minutes, stirring occasionally. Taste for seasoning.

Brown Sauce, Quick Method

| 1½ tablespoons butter | 2 cups beef bouillon |
| 1½ tablespoons flour | |

Melt butter in a heavy saucepan; add flour. Cook slowly over low heat, stirring occasionally, until it is thoroughly blended and about the color of a brown paper bag. Gradually add the beef bouillon. Bring the sauce to a boil and cook for 5 minutes, stirring constantly. Lower the heat and simmer the sauce gently for 30 minutes, stirring occasionally. Skim off the fat and strain the sauce through a fine sieve.

Baked Hominy Grits with Cheese

This ought to have another name in case the word grits gives you an uneasy feeling. It's lovely, light, nutty and flavorful. How else can I tell you to try it without singing a chorus of Sewanee.

❀

1 cup quick hominy grits	1 cup medium sharp Cheddar
4 cups boiling water	cheese, grated
1 teaspoon salt	3 tablespoons butter
Dash Tabasco	1 cup milk
2 eggs, well beaten	

Add grits to boiling salted water. Cover; cook over low flame for 15 minutes—it will be a good mush texture. Add salt, Tabasco, and let cool a little. Add milk and stir well. Add grated cheese, beat, then add 3 tablespoons butter, beating after each tablespoon. Add eggs and beat until smooth. Taste for seasoning—you may need more salt and a little pepper.

Pour into well-buttered baking dish. Sprinkle with a little finely grated cheese (optional). Bake in preheated 375° oven for 45 minutes, until puffy and golden brown. Serve immediately.

Serves 6.

Baked Pork and Beans

As you will observe, this one takes a while—but it's worth it.

❀

4 cups white beans (2 pounds)	1 cup molasses
2 tablespoons dry mustard	2 tablespoons brown sugar
1 pound unsliced bacon or salt pork	1 bottle catsup
2 onions, whole	1 cup whole tomatoes
2 cloves garlic, whole	¼ pound butter

Put the beans, which have been soaked over night, in a heavy Dutch oven with 2 tablespoons dry mustard and water to cover. Cook for 15 minutes. Pour into baking dish over the unsliced bacon or salt pork. Add onions, garlic, remaining dry mustard, molasses, brown sugar, catsup and tomatoes. Cook covered in a very slow oven (250°) for about 24 to 28 hours. The last two hours of cooking, uncover, and about 15 minutes before serving, add butter. Stir from bottom to prevent burning. If they start getting too dry, add water mixed with a little brown sugar.

Serves 12 to 14.

Red Beans and Rice

If you're serving a light meat course, this one is great for your starch. If it's for a luncheon, it's really all you need except for a light green salad with French dressing and a fresh fruit for dessert.

2 large onions, chopped
4 small scallions, chopped
2 cloves garlic, finely chopped
3 tablespoons bacon fat
1 tablespoon butter
1 green pepper, finely chopped
2 8-ounce cans tomato sauce
1 can water

2 whole, fresh tomatoes, coarsely
   chopped
4 cans (#300 size) red kidney
   beans
1 teaspoon salt
½ teaspoon red pepper flakes
1 heaping tablespoon chili powder

Sauté onions, scallions and garlic in bacon fat and butter until lightly browned. Add tomato sauce, water, tomatoes and green pepper and simmer for 30 minutes. Drain kidney beans and run water over them to get rid of the sweet flavored liquid in which the beans are packed. Add kidney beans, salt, red pepper flakes and chili powder. Cook very slowly 45 minutes or longer. Taste for seasoning. This can cook for 2 hours and only gets better if reheated the next day. Serve with steamed white rice.

Serves 10.

Potatoes à la Stockholm

I've never had anything quite like these potatoes. I first had them at the Stallmästaregarden in Stockholm in a lovely, lovely garden restaurant. I've tried many different ways of reproducing the recipe. This one seems to come the closest. It sounds like a lot of trouble, but believe me it's worth it!

❀

4 White Rose boiling potatoes, peeled and uniformly sliced thin—1/16 inch	Salt
	Black pepper, freshly ground
	Sprig of dill
Ice water	Butter
Milk	

Place potatoes in ice water to cover. Set for an hour or so in refrigerator. Remove from water, pat with towel to get rid of as much moisture as possible. Put potatoes in top of double boiler with salt, milk to cover, and a sprig of dill. Precook 15 minutes.

In buttered shallow baking dish, place potato slices carefully, allowing them to just overlap—it's better to use 2 or 3 baking dishes or even a pie plate, oven-proof if possible, so that they can be fresh and hot each time they're passed around. If baking dish is used, make it a long rectangular one and arrange potatoes in overlapping rows lengthwise. If you are using a round baking dish, arrange in a series of circles with potatoes overlapping—one layer—do not pile in deep layers like au gratin potatoes. Anyway, spoon some milk in which potatoes have been precooked over the slices, grind black pepper over whole, dot generously with butter, and bake in preheated 350° oven for 20 minutes. Serve immediately. If you use more than one baking dish, don't cook them all at the same time. Stagger baking by putting the second pan in the oven 10 minutes after the first and letting it cook for 20 minutes. Place third pan in oven 10 minutes after second and let it cook for 20 minutes, etc. There's a chance, if you serve enough of these, you'll never get to talk to your guests—but they'll say nice things about you and your potatoes.

Serves 4 to 6.

Crusty Sweet Potato Puffs

Serve these for Thanksgiving or Christmas dinner or some other special occasion. They look pretty, taste delectable, and aren't as sweet as you might expect.

❧

3 large sweet potatoes
1 tablespoon butter
Cream to moisten
½ teaspoon salt

Dash of nutmeg
Cornflakes, coarsely crushed
1 egg
Water

Boil potatoes, peel, rice and mash well. Then mix with butter and cream. Add seasoning. Chill. Roll into little balls about an inch or a little more in diameter. When rolled into balls, dip in egg beaten with a little water. Roll in crushed cornflakes. Bake in a greased pan in moderate oven, 350°, until crisp and brown or fry in deep fat.

You can roll the potato balls much easier if they are chilled so I do everything up to the rolling the night before.

Serves 6 to 8.

Cheese Stuffed Baked Potatoes

4 small baking potatoes
½ cup sour cream or milk (more or less, depending on the size of your potatoes)
½ cup Cheddar or Swiss cheese cut in small cubes

¼ cup grated Cheddar or Swiss cheese
4 tablespoons butter
¼ cup crisp fried, minced bacon
Salt and pepper
Cooking oil

Scrub the baking potatoes and rub oil on the skins. Bake in 450° preheated oven until done. Press gently with your fingers to check—about 30 to 45 minutes should do it. Cut baking potatoes in half, scoop out shells. Mix well, then add butter, salt, pepper, milk or sour cream and bacon bits. When a little cool, fold in cheese cubes. Pile high in potato shells. (You can do this much in the morning.)

Just before serving sprinkle with grated cheese and bake in 350° oven for about 25 minutes to heat through thoroughly and melt cheese cubes inside.

Serves 8.

Deep Fried Rice and Cheese Balls

2 eggs
2 cups cooked white rice (cold)
4 ounces mozzarella cheese, cut
    in ½-inch cubes (about 1 cup)

¾ cup fine dry bread crumbs
Vegetable oil or shortening for
    deep frying

Beat the eggs lightly with a fork until they are just combined. Then add the rice and stir gently but thoroughly, taking care not to mash it. Scoop up 1 tablespoon of the mixture in a spoon, place a cube of mozzarella in the middle, and top with another spoonful of rice. Press the two spoons together or use your hands to shape a ball. Roll the ball in bread crumbs and place on wax paper. Similarly, shape other balls. The balls may be fried at once, but they are easier to handle if refrigerated for 30 minutes.

Heat the oil in a deep-fat fryer to 375°. Preheat the oven to 250°, line a large baking dish with paper towels and put the dish in the oven. Fry the balls, 4 or 5 at a time, for about 5 minutes until they are golden brown and the cheese has melted. Transfer to the baking dish to drain. They may be kept warm in the oven for 10 minutes or so if they must wait, but no longer.

Serves 4 to 6.

Vegetables

◆

String Beans Greek Style

Back in the days when George was under contract to Twentieth Century Fox, we were in New York on one occasion when Mrs. Spyros Skouras, wife of Fox's Chairman of the Board, invited us out to their Long Island estate for the weekend.

She served some truly unusual dishes. One of the most memorable was these flavorful string beans. (An unusual string bean dish should be cherished—it's that rare.)

◆

4 medium onions, finely chopped	Salt to taste
4 large tomatoes, sliced	Cayenne pepper to taste
3 cloves garlic, finely chopped	2 pounds string beans

Brown onions and garlic in a little bacon drippings or oil until light golden brown. Add sliced tomatoes. Cook until well done. Add salt and cayenne pepper to taste. Cook string beans in salted water 10 minutes, drain well. Pour sauce over, cover, and cook slowly over low heat for one hour. Uncover last 15 minutes.

Serves 8 to 10.

Vegetable Gumbo Creole

This is a real staple around my house. It's another one of those accommodating gems that only improve with stretching, reheating and reassembling. It's got rhythm! Who could ask for anything more?

❧

2 packages frozen okra (or 1
    pound of fresh okra), cut
    crosswise
2 packages frozen lima beans
2 green peppers, chopped
4 medium tomatoes, sliced
    crosswise

2 packages frozen corn (or 8 ears
    of fresh corn, cut off cob)
1 small bunch of celery, coarsely
    chopped
Bread crumbs
Butter

Partially cook lima beans in salted water and then add corn. Add green peppers, okra and celery and cook until just done. Drain.

Place a layer of the vegetable mixture (reserve part of okra for top layer) in a buttered and crumbed baking dish. Then add a layer of tomatoes. Season with salt and pepper, dot with butter and bread crumbs. Repeat until casserole is filled. On top place a layer of okra that has been dipped in bread crumbs and sautéed in a little butter. Cover with bread crumbs and dot with butter. Bake in a 300° oven for about 1 hour. It can be cooked in the morning and reheated slowly before serving. It's even better the second day.

Serves 8 to 10.

Ratatouille

What's the best method known to man for cleaning out a vegetable bin? And the perfect stretch dish when you expect a number of people, and more than that keep arriving? The answer to both questions is Ratatouille.

Last time I made it I stripped the bin clean. I used three zuc-
chinis, two crook-neck squash, two green squash, one cucumber, half
an eggplant, four tomatoes, an onion, some celery, some leftover
string beans, asparagus, half a pound of mushrooms—and a partridge
in a pear tree.

The fact that it lets you clean out your larder may be the reason
French women favor this dish. Another good reason is when your
daughter, like mine, suddenly announces she's no longer a meat eater
—a strict vegetarian and she's so slim you're a nervous wreck about
her—you can give her an acre of this. It's tasty, nourishing, healthy and
pure—even her guru would approve.

❧

2 onions, thinly sliced
2 cloves garlic, crushed with a
    little salt
4 zucchinis, not peeled and sliced
1 cucumber, peeled and sliced
2 small eggplants, peeled and
    diced
2 green peppers, cut in strips
2 carrots, sliced
3 stalks celery, sliced

Fresh corn, cut off cob (optional)
½ pound green beans, cut in
    French style
6 tomatoes, peeled and sliced
Monosodium glutamate
Salt and pepper to taste
Sesame seeds (optional)
Whatever else suits your fancy—
    vegetable only, please

Parboil celery in salted water; add string beans. When both are done, drain. In a large shallow pan, sauté the onions and green peppers in oil until just soft. Add salt and pepper and a little monosodium glutamate. Add remaining vegetables, together with the drained parboiled beans and celery. Season again if necessary (it will be) and then add sesame seeds. Cover and cook the ratatouille over very low heat for about 1 hour, or until vegetables are very tender. Check the seasoning. (I like this kind of peppery.) Serve hot.

Serves 8 to 10 as a side dish.

Vegetable Pie

This is a really pretty one for your buffet.

❀

1 eggplant, peeled and sliced
   crosswise ¼ inch thick
3 large tomatoes, peeled and
   sliced ¼ inch thick
1 ear fresh corn, cooked for
   approximately 2 minutes and
   cut off cob before placing in
   pie, or frozen corn (optional)

2 onions, cut in ¼-inch rings
1 fresh green pepper, sliced
4 tablespoons Parmesan or
   Romano cheese
2 teaspoons garlic, crushed or
   chopped
Salt and pepper
Oil

Have an unsweetened, unbaked 10- to 11-inch flaky pie crust. Sprinkle pie crust with 2 tablespoons Parmesan or Romano cheese.

In a skillet, sauté the onion rings in a little hot oil until lightly brown. Add the eggplant and tomatoes and sauté until slightly soft.

Layer the vegetables in the pie crust; first the eggplant, tomatoes, half of the corn, onions and ending with the fresh green pepper. Sprinkle with a little oil or dot with butter and add more Parmesan or Romano cheese mixed with the garlic. Salt and pepper generously. Add an additional layer of the same vegetables; sprinkle again with a little oil or dot with butter and add more Parmesan or Romano cheese mixed with garlic. Bake in a preheated 350° oven about 40 to 45 minutes until vegetables are tender and the crust is golden brown.

Serves 8.

Artichoke Hearts with Hollandaise Sauce

2 cups canned artichoke hearts,
   heated in juice

Hollandaise sauce
Curry powder

Put heated artichoke hearts in shallow oven-proof baking dish. Cover with Hollandaise sauce (easy on the lemon). Sprinkle with curry powder. Place under broiler close to flame until it bubbles and is a little brown. Serve immediately in same baking dish.

Serves 4 to 6.

Quick Hollandaise Sauce

    3 egg yolks
    2 tablespoons lemon juice (scant)
    ¼ teaspoon salt

    Dash of cayenne
    ½ cup hot butter or margarine,
       melted

In a blender, combine egg yolks, lemon juice, salt and cayenne. Cover; turn blender on and off; remove cover. Turn blender to high speed; gradually add butter in a steady stream. Turn blender off. Serve immediately, or keep warm by placing blender container in 2 inches of hot (not boiling) water.

    Yields 1 cup.

Asparagus Polonaise

Select two bunches of large asparagus. Peel asparagus and discard the tough bottom portion. (Save it for broths and soups or for flavoring cream of asparagus soup.) Cut remaining asparagus crosswise into 1½-inch pieces. A slight angle is more attractive instead of straight across. Place asparagus in a deep fat fryer basket, a colander with a handle or a large deep strainer. Drop into kettle of rapidly boiling salted water and cook until just done (about 5 minutes). Lift out and place in individual portions on a warmed platter. Pour Polonaise Sauce over each portion, reserving a little extra sauce for the table. Garnish each portion with a little strip of pimento.

    Serves 6 to 8.

Polonaise Sauce

    ½ cup sweet butter
    ¼ cup soft bread crumbs
    2 small hard-boiled eggs, finely
       chopped

    1 tablespoon parsley, finely
       chopped
    Salt and pepper to taste

In a saucepan, melt the butter. When the butter foams, stir in the soft bread crumbs and continue to cook over low heat until the crumbs are well browned. Remove the pan from the heat and stir in the eggs and parsley. Add salt and pepper to taste.

Cauliflower with Cheese Sauce

Trim a large head of cauliflower, removing outer leaves and part of the core and cutting off any blemishes. Score the core with a knife to facilitate cooking. Place in a kettle of boiling salted water to cover and add 1 teaspoon lemon juice. Cover and simmer 25 to 30 minutes or until just tender when tested with a fork. Do not overcook. Cauliflower may be broken into flowerets and cooked for a shorter time.

Cover with Cheese Sauce.

Serves 6.

Cheese Sauce

3 tablespoons butter or part
    bacon drippings
3 tablespoons flour
¼ teaspoon dry mustard
Dash cayenne

3 cups + 3 tablespoons milk
2 cups grated sharp Cheddar
    cheese
Salt and pepper

Melt butter, stir in flour mixed with mustard. Heat milk if necessary, or add slowly if cold, stirring constantly to flour-mustard-butter mixture. Stir until it starts to thicken. Add salt and pepper. Then add cheese, stirring slowly and constantly until cheese melts. Taste for seasoning. Add more salt, pepper and a dash more dry mustard if desired (careful here). I use a little sprinkle of cayenne too. Great for cauliflower.

It's okay to cook it in the morning and reheat in double boiler.

This dish can be served with Polonaise Sauce (page 135) for a change.

Cabbage and Pine Nuts

You wouldn't think Dina Merrill Robertson would have spent much time slaving over a hot stove, but her small dinner parties always contain some delightful surprise like, for instance, the following cabbage recipe. Ordinarily I'd take a small helping of cabbage to assuage my hostess's feelings, but in this case I went back for seconds and thirds.

❧

1 head of cabbage
Handful of sugar (never mind your glove size)
Handful of salt
¼ cup butter

¼ cup toasted pignolas or pine nuts
¼ cup minced thick bacon, crisply cooked
Freshly ground pepper

As Dina tells it, you tear a small head of cabbage into individual leaves. Put them in a large pot, cover with water, throw in the handful of sugar and the handful of salt and allow to sit for 3 or 4 hours.

Before serving, drain, barely cover with water. Add a pinch of sugar, salt and freshly ground pepper. Cook only 5 minutes, drain and place in a warm serving dish. Pour about ¼ cup of melted butter over all and serve with a generous amount of the crisply cooked, minced bacon and toasted pignolas.

Serves 4.

Carrot Purée

2 pounds carrots, scraped and sliced
½ teaspoon sugar
½ teaspoon salt

⅓ cup butter
Black pepper, freshly ground
Dash of lemon juice
Parsley, finely chopped

Cover the carrots with water and add sugar and salt. Cook them, covered, over low heat for about 15 minutes, or until all the water has been absorbed and the carrots are tender. Add butter, mash the carrots, and season them with freshly ground black pepper and a dash of lemon juice. Pile the purée into a serving dish and sprinkle liberally with finely chopped parsley.

Serves 4 to 6.

Corn in Lettuce Leaf

If your corn is not just off the vine—and whose is?—or if it's been sitting in the market or if you have had it in the refrigerator a few days, this makes it taste like the way you remembered it but probably never was anyway.

❀

6 ears corn	Salt; pepper
6 large lettuce leaves	Melted butter or margarine

Dip the shucked and cleaned ear of corn in melted butter or margarine. Sprinkle with salt and pepper. Wrap the ear in a leaf of lettuce and then in aluminum foil. Bake in a 400° oven 30 to 40 minutes.

Celery-Carrot Sauté

4 carrots	4 stalks celery

Clean and slice the carrots. Strip any tough strings from the stalks of celery. Slice thinly on a slant with a sharp knife. Split wider, pale ends lengthwise. Mix with carrots.

Heat 1 tablespoon oil in heavy pan. Add carrots and celery. Keeping heat high, stir and fry about 2 minutes. Add ⅓ cup boiling water, about ½ teaspoon salt and ¼ teaspoon sugar. Cover tightly. When water boils, turn heat low and simmer until tender but crisp (7 to 10 minutes). Add a tablespoon of butter, if you wish, but you really don't need it. Serve at once.

Serves 6.

Salads
and
Salad
Dressings

Vegetable Salad

For people who are bored with vegetables and hardly ever take them when they are served, this is a lovely way to entice them. It's colorful and really tasty. I serve this salad to all my meat and potato tennis players and there's never any left. Need I say more.

❡

1 small cauliflower, broken into flowerets
1 pound fresh string beans, French cut
6 medium carrots, cut in strips
5 stalks celery, cut in half and then in strips
1 green pepper, cut in strips (optional)
4 small zucchinis, cut in strips or thin slices, unpeeled
Parsley, chopped

Monosodium glutamate
Salt and pepper
Tarragon
Lemon juice
Oil
6 or 8 medium-sized fresh mushrooms, sliced
Sweet onions or scallions (or any raw vegetable you like)
Pimento
Mayonnaise
A little fresh dill (optional)

Cook cauliflower, carrots, celery, green pepper and string beans in salted boiling water to which you have added monosodium glutamate. Cook until barely done. Just before the string beans (which should be added a little after the carrots, celery and green pepper because they take a little shorter time to cook) are cooked, add the zucchini and whatever other fresh vegetables are in season that need very little cooking.

Drain, chill and sprinkle with salt, pepper, a little more monosodium glutamate, tarragon, parsley, lemon juice and oil or French dressing. When ready to serve, check the seasoning. Add mushrooms and whatever raw vegetable you like for texture and flavor, such as sweet onions, scallions, cucumber strips and pimento (or leave your zucchini raw and add now). Toss with mayonnaise until well coated. Sprinkle with parsley and a little fresh dill (if you have it) and serve.

Almost any fresh vegetable you like can be used in this—leftovers or otherwise. The big trick is not to overcook any of them, but to use a combination of textures, flavors and colors—I've used a few cold sliced potatoes or hard-boiled eggs.

Serves 14.

Italian Salad

This is called Italian Salad because it has garbanzo beans and sliced Italian salami. It could be called Jewish salad if you use chick peas and kosher salami or Mexican if you use pinto beans and chorizos.

❧

1 clove garlic, cut in half
1 small can artichoke hearts,
    cut in quarters
1 head Bibb lettuce
½ cucumber, sliced thin
1 green pepper, cut in wide strips
1 sweet red onion
1 small can garbanzo beans,
    drained
4 slices Italian salami, sliced thin

3 fresh mushrooms, chopped
    (optional)
4 radishes, sliced thin
1 small tomato, quartered
Salt
Monosodium glutamate
Fresh black pepper, coarsely
    ground
Pinch of tarragon

Rub a salad bowl with cut side of garlic clove. Marinate the cucumbers, green pepper strips, garbanzo beans, artichoke hearts, radishes and the small tomato in the bowl in ½ recipe of French Dressing (page 148) Cover bowl with plastic wrap, set in refrigerator and let chill until you are ready to serve.

Just before serving add lettuce, onions, Italian salami and fresh mushrooms. Sprinkle with a little salt, monosodium glutamate, pepper and a pinch of tarragon and remainder of dressing. Toss very lightly. Squeeze a little lemon over salad and serve ice-cold.

Serves 6 to 8.

More Than Potato Salad

I saw David Wade prepare this on a television show. I tried it and it really should be called Elixir or Ambrosia of Potato Salad—not just Potato Potato Salad.

❧

3 or 4 cups hot cooked potatoes, diced
1½ cups coarsely shredded cabbage
½ cup grated carrots, uncooked
2 tablespoons green pepper, finely minced
1 teaspoon salt
1 teaspoon pepper
1 tablespoon Dijon mustard

2 tablespoons peanut or safflower oil
1 tablespoon white wine vinegar
2 tablespoons fresh onion, finely grated
½ cup sliced ripe olives
½ cup mild dill pickle, chopped
2 tablespoons pimento, chopped
⅔ cup mayonnaise

While the potatoes are still warm, blend in a large mixing bowl with all the other ingredients and chill.

Serves 8 to 10.

Salad Niçoise

Missy discovered this one—when she discovered beautiful room service in beautiful Paris. I think she first ordered it because it had tuna fish in it—but when mom got a taste of it, it was forever after a perfect whole meal salad—without lettuce imagine!

❧

1 2-ounce can anchovies, drained
2 hard-boiled eggs, sliced
2 medium tomatoes, cut in wedges
1 pound cooked green beans, cut French style
1 green pepper, cut in strips
8 ripe olives, pitted

2 potatoes, boiled and sliced crosswise ½ inch thick
1 sweet onion, cut in thin slices
1 6½-ounce can tuna, drained and broken into bite-sized wedges
French dressing (page 148)

142

Marinate green beans in French dressing in refrigerator over night, if possible. Chill remaining ingredients. Place all ingredients in a large, chilled salad bowl. When ready to serve, pour French dressing over and toss lightly, but thoroughly, being careful not to break up tuna too much.

Serves 8.

Mother's Chicken Salad

This is chicken salad as my mother used to make it. It is unusually good, and I use it ofen. It keeps well for a couple of days.

One suggestion: If you're going to keep it, don't add the unsweetened whipped cream until you're ready to serve.

❧

Meat of 2 tender, plump cooked
chickens, cut into cubes
2 cups chopped celery
½ cup chopped green pepper
2 teaspoons grated onion
(optional)
¾ cup chopped nuts (pecans
preferable)
4 hard-boiled eggs

Salt and pepper to taste
1 tablespoon Worcestershire sauce
Tabasco sauce
Capers
⅔ cup mayonnaise
½ cup unsweetened whipped
cream
French dressing

Marinate meat for several hours with French dressing, then drain, if necessary. Add celery, peppers, chopped eggs, salt, pepper and grated onion. Stir gently over and over to mix well, then add Worcestershire, Tabasco, nuts, then mayonnaise, then capers. Stir gently to mix well.

Just before serving add ½ cup unsweetened whipped cream to mayonnaise.

Serves 14.

Curried Chicken Salad

1 cup coconut, shredded
1 cup bleached raisins, cooked
1 cup peanuts, chopped
1 cup bananas, diced
1 cup apples, diced
1 cup celery, diced

2 cups cooked chicken, diced
2 tablespoons curry powder
1 cup chutney
¼ to ½ cup mayonnaise
Salt to taste

Add the mayonnaise to the above ingredients and season to taste. Chill over night.

Serves 16.

Bessie's and Mr. Hansen's Danish Cucumbers

My sister, Bessie, is an incredible lady. Her range of interests is infinite. Her convictions are strong. Her philosophy is beautiful. Her cooking is superb. She is also persistent. For some time she tried to unearth the recipe for cucumbers that have the distinctive flavor of the ones they serve at Scandia, one of Los Angeles' top restaurants. She did everything ingenuity and the law would allow to zero in on it. My brother-in-law, the charmer, got it the hard way—he asked Mr. Hansen, the owner of Scandia, for it and here it is.

*

3 large cucumbers, peeled and
   sliced thin
⅓ cup white vinegar

1 tablespoon salt
1½ teaspoon sugar
¼ teaspoon pepper

Let the cucumbers stand with salt at least 1 hour or over night, if possible. A plate should be placed on top of the cucumbers and weighted.

Drain and rinse well with cold water. While draining, mix the white vinegar with the sugar and pepper. Taste. Pour over the cucumbers and let them stand at least 2 hours.

Serves 6 as a side dish.

Cucumbers in Dilled Sour Cream

3 or 4 cucumbers, peeled and sliced
1 part vinegar and 1 part water,
   enough to cover cucumbers
1 tablespoon sugar
2 cups sour cream

Salt and pepper
2 tablespoons lemon juice
2 tablespoons tarragon vinegar
½ cup fresh dill, chopped
2 green onions, finely chopped

Marinate the cucumbers in the vinegar, water, salt and sugar for at least 1 or 2 hours. Drain thoroughly. Mix remaining ingredients together and stir in the drained cucumbers. Chill until ready to serve.

To prepare ahead of time: The cucumbers can be marinated the day before and the sour cream mixture can be combined the day before. The two can be combined in the morning of the day on which they are to be served. Keep them refrigerated until time to serve.

This one is really good with yellow onions sliced fairly thin—⅛ inch—in which case marinate the onions with the cucumbers. And instead of fresh dill, which is hardly ever around when you need it, add ½ teaspoon dill weed to sour cream mixture.

Serves 6 as a side dish.

Finger Salad

A salad without vinegar or lemon juice—really unusual—try it—and by all means eat it with your fingers.

4 tablespoons oil
2 teaspoons monosodium
   glutamate
2 cloves garlic, cut in half

1 head romaine lettuce
Salt
2 tablespoons tarragon
¼ cup parsley, finely chopped

Place oil in salad bowl. Add monosodium glutamate and garlic cloves. Let soak together for 15 minutes. Remove the garlic and add romaine which has been chilled. Add salt and sprinkle tarragon and parsley. Turn leaves carefully and quickly so as to coat each leaf, but do not let them get soft or wilted.

Use only the choicest small center leaves. Mix just before serving. Serves 4 to 6.

Louise's Marinated String Beans

4 16-ounce cans whole string beans
Sweet, dried basil
Medium ground, fresh pepper

Lettuce
Basic French Dressing (page 148)
  (double the amount)

Drain cans of string beans. Place layer of beans in shallow dish. Cover with Basic French Dressing. Sprinkle very liberally with sweet basil and pepper. Repeat layering. Marinate in refrigerator, over night if possible, turning occasionally. Drain excess dressing and serve on lettuce beds.

Serves 10 to 12.

Bea's Wilted Spinach Salad

1 pound fresh spinach
12 slices bacon, diced
6 tablespoons hot bacon fat
2 tablespoons oil

3 tablespoons red wine vinegar
Juice of ½ lemon
Salt to taste
Pepper, freshly cracked, to taste

Wash and drain the spinach leaves. Cut away the tough stems and discard. Tear into bite-sized pieces and place in a large bowl. Cook the bacon until crisp. Remove the bacon with a slotted spoon and drain on paper toweling. Crumble and add to greens in bowl. Add the oil, vinegar, lemon, salt and pepper to the bacon fat. Heat and stir. Pour mixture over spinach greens and toss well. Serve immediately. Don't try holding this one for anybody.

Serves 8.

Sour Cream Cheese Fruit Salad Mold

When television was "live from Hollywood" each Sunday evening after my show we'd gather at my home to see the broadcast out here three hours later and eat one of Pauline's great dinners. One of the highlights was this lovely molded fruit salad. Pauline could make this ahead and we could all watch the show together, comfortably reassured that at least for one more week nothing catastrophic had happened, or at least the show got on and off between NBC peacocks. If I forgot the lyric to my favorite ballad or I danced left when all the dancers went right, the sight of this salad would soothe my battered ego.

❀

1 tablespoon gelatine
1 package red Jello (raspberry if possible)
2 3-ounce packages cream cheese
2 ½-pint cartons sour cream
½ of a 2-ounce jar pimentos

1 cup celery, chopped
½ cup blanched, slivered and toasted almonds
2 cups canned Royal Anne cherries (pitted)
1 14-ounce can crushed pineapple (drained)

Dressing

Sour cream
Mayonnaise

Orange or the pineapple juice drained above

Beat together 1 package of cream cheese and ½-pint carton of sour cream. Gradually add Jello which has been dissolved according to directions on the package, using fruit juices instead of water. Then add gelatine. Add pineapple, nuts, pimento, celery and cherries.

Combine, in equal parts, sour cream and mayonnaise for the dressing. Thin with fruit juice and add a little powdered sugar if necessary.

Garnish with Cream Cheese Nut Balls.

Serves 8 to 10.

Cream Cheese Nut Balls

Mix cream cheese with a little cream, Worcestershire sauce and Tabasco sauce. Roll into small balls, then in crushed nuts. Garnish around mold. If ring mold is used, place nut balls in center of mold.

Pauline's French Dressing

1½ cups oil
½ cup vinegar
2 teaspoons salt
1 teaspoon pepper
1 teaspoon sugar

1 tablespoon onion, grated
1 clove garlic, cut in half (for
    stronger garlic flavor, mash
    garlic in press)

Combine all ingredients in a jar and shake well.

Before assembling salad, sprinkle salt and pepper, or juice of ½ lemon or lime if you have it, over greens. Toss lightly—add dressing—toss lightly but thoroughly.

This keeps very well. I generally make this amount, keeping it in the refrigerator in a good tall jar and using what I need when I need it. Shake the jar before pouring out ½ cupful, which is about what you need for tossing a salad for 4 people. Add more dressing to the jar from time to time—the garlic flavors the oil and it really gets better.

Yields about 2 cups.

Basic French Dressing

6 tablespoons good fresh olive oil
2 tablespoons wine vinegar
1 tablespoon fresh lemon juice
1 teaspoon salt

½ teaspoon black pepper,
    coarsely ground
1 clove garlic, pressed

Combine the above ingredients in a tall jar. Shake well before serving.
Yields enough dressing for 6 salads.

Vinaigrette Dressing

6 tablespoons oil
Juice of ½ lemon
2 tablespoons wine vinegar
2 tablespoons sweet red pepper,
   chopped
1 teaspoon green olives, finely
   chopped (optional)
1 teaspoon pimento, chopped
1 teaspoon gherkins, finely
   chopped

1 teaspoon capers, finely chopped
1 teaspoon chives, finely chopped,
   or ½ teaspoon onion juice
1 teaspoon parsley, finely chopped
Yolk of 1 hard-boiled egg,
   finely chopped
1 teaspoon salt
1 teaspoon pepper
Paprika

Mix all ingredients together. Use for cold fish, meat and vegetables. Great over chilled canned asparagus or chilled fresh cooked asparagus, broccoli or cauliflower.

   Yields 4 portions.

Jody's Favorite Russian Dressing

1 cucumber, peeled, finely chopped, and placed on paper toweling to drain
3 stalks celery, finely chopped
½ green pepper, finely chopped
2 hard-boiled eggs, finely chopped

Salt and pepper to taste
1 cup Miracle Whip
2 heaping tablespoons chili sauce or catsup
1 teaspoon Worcestershire sauce
Dash of Tabasco sauce

Mix vegetables and eggs. Salt and pepper to taste. Mix chili sauce, Worcestershire sauce, Tabasco sauce and mayonnaise. Stir in vegetables.

Serve over hearts of lettuce cut in portion-sized wedges.

Yields enough dressing for 6 salads.

For Closers

❧

Desserts and Pies

Cakes and Cookies

Desserts and Pies

◆

Apple Pot

6 firm medium baking apples	Pinch of salt
Cinnamon	Lemon juice
Sugar	Maple or light brown sugar
Butter	Black walnuts or broken pecan
½ pint whipping cream	halves

Pare, core and slice apples. Place apple slices in a buttered baking dish and sprinkle each layer generously with cinnamon and sugar. Dot each layer generously with butter. Continue layering with apples until dish is nearly full. Then prepare:

Crumbly Mixture

½ cup butter	1 teaspoon cinnamon
1 cup sugar	½ teaspoon salt
¾ cup flour	

Combine the flour, sugar, butter, cinnamon and salt into a crumbly mixture. Sprinkle this thickly over the apples. Bake in a 350° oven until the apples are tender and the top is crusty and glazed. Serve hot (better) or cold with a bowl of whipped cream which is whipped lightly with a pinch of salt, lemon juice and maple or light brown sugar. Sprinkle black walnuts or broken pecan halves over the top.

Serves 8 to 10.

Apple Pancake

Whenever I think of this recipe I think of Sam Goldwyn, that great pioneer genius at movie making. Mr. Goldwyn was always in marvel-

ous condition. He walked miles every day and rigidly adhered to a diet of simple foods. It seemed to me he almost never ate anything for lunch other than cottage cheese and applesauce. Frances, his wife, conscientiously helped him stick to his diet.

One evening when we all happened to be visiting Palm Springs, the Goldwyns came over to our house for dinner. It was the dessert that made me nervous because quite honestly I had forgotten all about it. As the moment of truth and serving arrived, I desperately remembered an apple pancake I had had a couple of times at Lindy's in New York, for which the friendly chef had given me the recipe.

So I peeled and cored the apples I had on hand quickly, got out the sugar, butter, eggs, etc. I needed for the dish and started boldly on this Apple Pancake in front of the company. That takes nerve. At any rate in the middle of my elaborate prestidigitations, Frances Goldwyn announced calmly, "Sam won't have dessert." My spirits dropped but they needn't have. Sam Goldwyn ate my Apple Pancake. As a matter of fact, Sam Goldwyn ate one entire Apple Pancake! The dish was a smash. And to this day, when people gather on Broadway around the old show business haunts, they still talk in whispers about the night Sam Goldwyn threw caution and diet to the wind and ate a whole one of my Apple Pancakes.

If you think I've slightly hyperbolized the aforetold story, find your own neighborhood Sam Goldwyn and try your Apple Pancake on him—You'll see!

❦

3 tablespoons butter	1 large tart apple
1½ tablespoons brown sugar	3 eggs
1 tablespoon granulated sugar	½ cup milk (scant)

Melt butter in large skillet (Teflon, if possible). Add brown and granulated sugar and cook over medium high heat. Sugar will brown a little so be careful not to let it burn. Add apple sliced in thin wedges—spread evenly over skillet. Lower heat, let apples cook a little—like one or two minutes. While they are cooking, beat eggs with milk. Pour over all evenly. When eggs start to set a little, turn up heat to high. Check underside occasionally, lifting to make sure it isn't sticking. When crisp and brown underneath—it will still be slightly moist on top—invert on hot platter and serve immediately.

Serves 3 to 4.

Kleeman's Apple Pie

Most people complain that that great Southern cooking you hear so much about is never found in restaurants, except, of course, for New Orleans. You only taste it when you're lucky enough to be invited into someone's home. Kleeman's Restaurant in Nashville, Tennessee, was the exception—and I remember as a child anticipating for a whole week that Saturday luncheon with my father at Kleeman's.

I have two of their recipes in here. One is this incredible Apple Pie and another is the Chicken on Egg Bread (really Cornbread) on pages 90, 91.

❦

1 tablespoon flour
4 tablespoons butter, melted
½ teaspoon nutmeg
¾ cup orange juice

1 cup sugar
3 medium-sized very tart apples
   (Pippins), finely chopped
Unbaked pie crust

Stir flour into melted butter. To this add nutmeg, orange juice, sugar, and mix together. Place chopped apples in pastry shell and pour above ingredients over them. Put strips of pastry over top and bake for 15 minutes in 450° oven. Reduce heat to 300° and bake until done—usually 25-30 minutes. Use a well-greased 9-inch pie pan. I suggest using a pie crust recipe that calls for vegetable shortening, lard or butter, and ice water—or use your own favorite pastry recipe. Put pastry in refrigerator for at least 2 hours before using.

Serves 8.

Edana Romney's Fresh Plum Tart

Edana Romney gives lovely, legendary Sunday luncheons, and occasionally the recipes therefrom.

9-inch flaky pie crust, unbaked	6 heaping tablespoons sugar
8 medium-sized fresh plums,	¼ pound butter
halved and pitted	Sweetened whipped cream or
¾ cup almonds, coarsely ground	sour cream (optional)

Make a 9-inch flaky pie crust. In the unbaked pie crust, sprinkle on the bottom about 3 tablespoons almonds and 2 heaping tablespoons sugar. Place on the bottom of the pie crust the fresh plums, cut side up. Again sprinkle over the plums ½ cup almonds and the remaining sugar. Dot generously with butter (not margarine). Bake according to your pie crust recipe.

Serve with or without sweet or sour cream. Sprinkle with remaining toasted almonds. The almonds may be toasted by spreading them around on a cookie sheet and placing in a 400° preheated oven. Watch carefully to prevent burning.

Serves 6.

Fresh Peach Pie

Make this beautiful pie when peaches are in season.

❧

Coconut Almond Pie Crust

| 1 cup blanched almonds | ¼ cup sugar |
| 1 cup moist-style flaked coconut | ¼ cup butter or margarine |

Grind almonds medium fine. Mix with coconut. Work in sugar and butter with fingers or spoon. Press evenly in bottom and sides of a 9-inch glass pie plate, saving 3 tablespoons crumbly mixture for top. Bake in a 375° preheated oven until light golden brown. It should take about 10-12 minutes. If edges begin to get too brown, cover edges with aluminum foil, leaving center uncovered. Place remaining crumb mixture in a shallow pan and toast in the oven at the same time as pie shell. This should only take 5 minutes. (see next page)

Filling

1 cup sour cream (½-pint carton)	1 teaspoon vanilla
6 tablespoons powdered sugar	3 cups sliced fresh peaches
1 teaspoon orange juice	½ cup whipping cream
1 teaspoon shredded orange rind	Dash of salt

Beat sour cream. Add salt, 4 tablespoons powdered sugar, orange juice, orange rind and vanilla. Spread on bottom and sides of shell. Cover with peaches arranged in an attractive manner in pie shell. Whip cream; fold in remaining 2 tablespoons of powdered sugar. Cover peaches with whipped cream. Sprinkle toasted coconut mixture, reserved from pie shell, over top. Chill.

Serves 6.

—But when the peach season is over, use the Orange Pie filling in the Coconut Almond pie crust.

Orange Pie Filling

6 medium-sized fresh oranges, peeled carefully and sliced crosswise	⅔ cup apricot jam
	1½ cups orange juice
	3 tablespoons cornstarch
1 teaspoon vanilla	3 tablespoons toasted coconut
½ cup sugar	mixture, reserved from pie shell

Arrange orange slices in an attractive pattern in pie shell. Mix cornstarch with a little orange juice to form a thick paste. Blend with the rest of the orange juice in a saucepan. Add the sugar and apricot jam. Cook until thickened and translucent. Remove from heat and add vanilla. Spread toasted coconut mixture over orange slices in pie shell. Pour the syrup over the orange slices, coating them completely. Chill.

If you don't like coconut, make it with your favorite flaky pie crust and forget the coconut crumb topping. (Why wouldn't anybody like coconut?)

Serves 6.

Pecan Crunch Pie

I have a pen friend—her name is Mrs. Bernice Allen—she writes me wonderful letters often about many subjects I'm really interested in: politics, people, campus activities (her husband is a professor), books, music, plays, movies—ME! And occasionally she sends me a recipe. Here's a beaut—there's another one called Cheese Pit on page 118. They're both unusual, and have graduated from the tennis players (who eat everything—remember?) to the jet set, who eat hardly anything but love these.

◊

3 eggs
½ teaspoon baking powder
1 cup sugar
½ pint whipping cream

11 graham crackers
1 cup pecans, chopped
1 teaspoon vanilla

Beat eggs and baking powder. Add sugar very slowly. Beat until very stiff. Crush graham crackers. Add them and pecans (by folding) to egg mixture. Add vanilla. Spread in heavily buttered pie pan. Bake at 350° for 30 minutes. Chill at least 4 or 5 hours. Whip cream and spread on pie. Excellent!
   Serves 6.

Fudge Pie

½ cup butter
3 squares unsweetened chocolate
1 cup sugar
2 eggs

½ cup flour
Pinch of salt
1 teaspoon vanilla
½ cup pecans

Melt butter and chocolate together in double boiler. Cool. Add remaining ingredients and mix well. Pour into a 9-inch greased pie pan. Bake in a very slow, preheated (300°–325°) oven for 20 minutes. Cool and refrigerate. Serve with whipped cream or ice cream.
   Serves 6.

Crême Brulée

3 cups heavy cream
6 tablespoons sugar
6 egg yolks

2 teaspoons vanilla extract
½ cup light brown sugar

Pre-heat oven to slow 300°.

Heat the cream over boiling water and stir in the sugar. Beat the egg yolks until light and pour the hot cream over them gradually, stirring vigorously. Stir in the vanilla and strain the mixture into a baking dish. Place the dish in a pan containing one inch of hot water and bake until a silver knife inserted in the center comes out clean, or 35 minutes. Do not overbake; the custard will continue to cook from retained heat when it is removed from the oven. Chill thoroughly.

Before serving, cover the surface with the brown sugar. Set the dish on a bed of cracked ice and put the crême under the broiler until the sugar is brown and melted. Serve immediately.

Serves 6.

Cottage Cheese and Blueberry Pancakes

This is Jody's favorite—and I got it from Mr. Fritzel of Fritzel's Restaurant in Chicago. This can be a luncheon dish or a dessert.

❧

2 cups coarse cottage cheese
1 tablespoon lemon juice
¼ cup sugar

2 large eggs
1 cup flour
Pinch of salt

Whip cottage cheese until creamy. Add lemon juice, sugar, salt and eggs. Mix well. Add flour until batter is thick enough to fry like hot cakes. When ready to serve, melt butter in hot skillet. Drop batter from spoon and fry until crisp and golden brown like hot cakes. Serve it with blueberry sauce.

Heat fresh or frozen blueberries, add sugar to taste—keep hot. Place two hot cakes for each person on warmed dessert plate, pour blueberry sauce over them, and put a generous dab of sour cream on top. Serves 6.

Gingerbread with Caramel Sauce

Pauline makes this better than anybody. Anybody.

❀

1 cup molasses	2 eggs, beaten separately
2 teaspoons baking soda	½ cup sugar
1 teaspoon cinnamon	½ cup butter, melted
1 teaspoon ginger	2 cups flour (scant)
¼ teaspoon nutmeg	1 cup boiling water

Mix molasses, soda and spices. Add sugar, butter, flour and water; beat well. Add egg yolks and fold in whites. Pour in a greased ring mold and bake in a 350° oven 35 to 40 minutes. (Don't worry if batter seems thin, it's supposed to be.)

Caramel Sauce

2 egg yolks	1 tablespoon butter
1 cup cream	1 teaspoon vanilla
1 pound light brown sugar	⅛ teaspoon salt

Add egg yolks and cream to sugar. Cook until creamy in double boiler. Add butter. When cool, add vanilla and salt.

Serve this on a large round platter. I have a little silver bowl that fits right in the center of the ring after the gingerbread has been unmolded. Gingerbread and sauce are even nicer when served a little warm.

Serves 8.

Pots au Crême

These are easy to make—rich—very chocolate-y, but a lovely finale for any kind of dinner because you serve such tiny quantities of it. Louis Jourdan is a fine amateur chef. He tasted my testing of this one on several occasions and I think he gave me four crossed forks. The only trick is to watch it like you would an eight-month old baby handling his own spoon and oatmeal over your best carpet and take it off the heat before you think it's really done. It hardens as it chills and should have a very creamy texture.

Cook it carefully and lovingly. If you have two double boilers it helps.

◍

2 cups heavy cream	8 ounces dark sweet chocolate
¼ cup sugar	1 teaspoon vanilla
6 egg yolks	

Heat cream and sugar in one double boiler over low heat. Melt chocolate, stirring occasionally, in the other double boiler or just over hot water. Blend the sugar and chocolate very carefully, stirring constantly. Remove from heat. Beat egg yolks in a bowl and gradually pour into hot mixture, stirring constantly. Return to double boiler, stirring constantly until it begins to thicken. Don't leave it and above all, don't cook it too long. It gets much thicker when it chills. I would say 10 minutes is the maximum. Remove from the heat, stirring all the while. Add vanilla. Pour into demitasse cups or pots au crême. I have on occasion when it cools slightly added chocolate chips. If you have a thin crowd, serve a little dab of whipped cream on top. You have to eat this with a demitasse spoon or the smallest teaspoon you have.

Serves 8 to 10.

Prune Whip with Port Wine

½ pound dried prunes	1 cup port wine
Water	1 cup whipping cream

⅔ cup (scant) granulated sugar 1 tablespoon confectioners' sugar
3 lemon slices, with rind Slivered blanched almonds, toasted

Soak the prunes a couple of hours in water to cover. Drain. Place them in a saucepan and add the sugar, lemon slices with rind and water to cover. Bring to a boil and cook until the prunes are tender. Drain (saving the juice), leaving the prunes in the kettle. Add the port wine and cook 10 minutes longer. Remove the pits and put the prunes through a sieve, or purée in an electric blender. Add a little more port, or the juice in which prunes were cooked, if necessary to make the prunes moist.

Whip the cream and mix half of it with the prunes. Sweeten the remaining cream with confectioners' sugar and use it as a garnish. Top with almonds.

Because it is rich, I serve small portions in little crystal crème de menthe glasses or pots au crème—with the smallest teaspoons I have.
Serves 6.

Bea's Brownies

½ pound bitter chocolate 1½ cups sifted flour
1½ cups butter 3 teaspoons vanilla
6 eggs 1 cup nuts, chopped
3 cups sugar

Melt butter and chocolate in double boiler. Beat eggs, adding sugar slowly, then add melted chocolate and butter. Add flour, vanilla and nuts in that order. Bake in a preheated 350° oven in two 8-inch pans for 20 to 25 minutes. Don't let it overcook. It should be very moist in the center.

Serve this warm for dessert. Simply cut into larger portions and top with vanilla ice cream. Mmmm!
Yields approximately 48 Brownies.

Maple Walnut Ice Cream

My daughter, Missy, is beautiful, slim, sylphlike. She loves this ice cream and eats quantities of it. I use her as a shill occasionally for dishes like this one. Folks who ordinarily won't taste anything resembling ice cream figure they'll come out looking like her if they try it. It's Machiavellian, but it doesn't make enemies—just believers.

❧

2 qt. ice cream maker

1½ cups light cream	Pinch of salt
4 egg yolks	2 cups heavy whipping cream
½ cup maple syrup	½ cup walnuts, coarsely chopped

In the top of a double boiler scald light cream over direct heat. In a bowl, stir the maple syrup and salt with the beaten eggs. Gradually add the scalded cream, stirring constantly, and return the mixture to the top of the double boiler. Cook the mixture over simmering water, stirring constantly, until it is thickened. Let the custard cool.

Whip the heavy cream until it holds a shape and fold it into the cold custard. Add the walnuts. Pour the mixture into the freezer can with the dasher, cover it tightly, and lower it into the freezer, packed with alternating layers of cracked ice and rock salt in the proportion of approximately 1 cup salt to 6 cups ice. Connect the dasher with the crank mechanism and start the mixture turning by hand or electricity. When the ice cream is frozen, remove the can and wipe it carefully to remove any salt. Remove the dasher, press the ice cream down, and cover the can again. Drain off the salt water, return the can to the freezer, and repack with ice and salt until ready to serve.

Yields about two quarts.

Pauline's Coffee Ice Cream

2 qt. ice cream maker

2 cups sugar	6 egg yolks
1½ cups cold water	3 tablespoons instant coffee
1½ cups heavy cream	3 tablespoons brandy (optional
1½ cups milk	but nice)

In a saucepan dissolve sugar in water over medium heat. Bring to a boil and boil for 5 minutes. Let the syrup cool.

In a heavy saucepan or the top of a double boiler, combine heavy cream, milk, syrup and egg yolks. Stir the custard over medium heat or over hot water until it coats a spoon or spatula. Add instant coffee and combine it well with custard. Let the custard cool and strain it into the freezer can with the dasher. Cover it tightly, and lower it into the freezer, packed with alternating layers of cracked ice and rock salt in the proportion of approximately 1 cup salt to 6 cups ice. Connect the dasher with the crank mechanism and start the mixture turning by hand or by electricity. When the ice cream is frozen, remove the can and wipe it carefully to remove any salt. Remove the dasher, press the ice cream down, and cover the can again. Drain off the salt water, return the can to the freezer, and repack it with ice and salt until ready to serve.

Yields about two quarts.

Unfattening Strawberry Ice Cream

I don't like to sound pushy, but you must try the Maple Walnut and Pauline's Coffee Ice Cream. After you do, you'll be ready for my dietetic strawberry. I hadn't planned on including it in this book, but I served it once for my publisher and he had three helpings. He obviously is a man of impeccable taste since he 1) insisted I write this book and 2) went bananas over my diet strawberry ice cream.

There is a product called Dsertwhip, which is an unwhipped dessert topping that can fool almost anybody. I was sure it was whipped cream the first two or three times I tasted it. It isn't and it's so low on the calorie counter that you can have ice cream three times a day and be under your quota.

❖

2 qt. ice cream maker
1 carton (10.66 fluid ounces) Dsertwhip

1 package frozen strawberries or raspberries, artificially sweetened, or if you want to fudge a little, regular sweetener

Allow berries to thaw and then mash with a fork. Blend into Dsertwhip. Pour the mixture into the freezer can with the dasher, cover it tightly, and lower it into the freezer, packed with alternating layers of cracked ice and rock salt in the proportion of approximately 1 cup salt to 6 cups ice. Connect the dasher with the crank mechanism and start the mixture turning by hand or electricity. When the ice cream is frozen, remove the can and wipe it carefully to remove any salt. Remove the dasher, press·the ice cream down, and cover the can again. Drain off the salt water, return the can to the freezer, and repack it with ice and salt until ready to serve. Serve it soon—it doesn't seem to keep as well as regular ice cream, but you probably won't have any left over anyway.

Makes 1 quart.

English Rolled Wafers with Chocolate Fudge Sauce

½ cup molasses
½ cup butter
1 cup flour (scant)

⅔ cup sugar
1 tablespoon ginger
Ice cream

Heat molasses to boiling point, add butter, then slowly (stirring constantly) add flour mixed and sifted with ginger and sugar. Drop medium-sized portions from tip of cooking spoon on greased, inverted iron skillet or heavy, shallow baking dish. Space them two inches apart. Bake 15 minutes in a 300° oven. Cool slightly, remove from pan, and roll over handle of wooden spoon while warm so that the edges are barely touching and a cavity is formed. Just before serving fill each cavity with vanilla ice cream or coffee ice cream and pour Chocolate Fudge Sauce over the top of each wafer.

Serves 6 to 8.

Chocolate Fudge Sauce

1½-ounce square of chocolate	1 cup boiling water
1 tablespoon butter	1 cup sugar
2 tablespoons corn syrup	½ teaspoon vanilla
⅛ teaspoon salt	

Melt chocolate in a double boiler over hot water. Add butter, corn syrup, salt, boiling water and sugar, stirring constantly. Finish cooking over direct heat and boil for 3 minutes. Cool and add vanilla. Use it hot or cold or you may reheat it in a double boiler over boiling water.

Makes ¾ cup.

Rice Pudding from the Riviera Hotel

One night after that second show at the Riviera in Vegas, I sat down with a couple of hungry show folk and let me tell you—I'll put them up against any hungry group and that includes ball players, opera stars or lumberjacks. Vic Damone started the whole thing. He ordered rice pudding. Since he was playing the Flamingo, it was kind of a shocker for me to find that he came to the Riviera for his rice pudding, along with Shecky Greene and Don Rickles of the Sahara. It was great! I begged Mr. Gruber, Food Chief of the Riviera, for the recipe for Pauline and me.

He finally gave it to me—ten years later—and then only because of Lorne Greene, who was going to be a guest on my television show. Lorne had lost 60 pounds on that famous Duke University Rice Diet and I didn't want him to kick the rice habit cold turkey so I S.O.S.'d Mr. Gruber. Here's why he took ten years sending it to me. The recipe called for 6 pounds of rice, 60 eggs, 20 quarts of milk, etc. He broke it down to this:

❧

½ cup regular rice	½ cup sugar
1 cup water, salted	1 cup plump raisins
1 quart whole milk	½ teaspoon vanilla
⅛ pound (½ stick) butter	3 tablespoons sugar
3 eggs	1 tablespoon cinnamon

Pour rice slowly into rapidly boiling, slightly salted, water in a large pot. Do not stir. Cover tightly and cook exactly 7 minutes, at which time all the water will be absorbed and the rice will be slightly undone. Add the milk and butter. Stir a little. Bring to a boil, cover and cook slowly over a low flame for 1 hour.

Meanwhile, beat eggs; add sugar, raisins and vanilla. Pour the mixture into the rice, stirring slowly until the rice starts to thicken. Serve hot, warm or cold with a mixture of cinnamon and sugar sprinkled lightly and evenly over the top.

This should serve 4 people, unless they're show folk, in which case it will serve 2.

Very Chocolate-y Soufflé

8 ounces dark sweet chocolate	1 teaspoon powdered instant coffee
¼ cup sugar	Pinch of cinnamon
4 eggs, separated	Confectioners' sugar
1 ounce rum	

In top of a double boiler over hot water, melt chocolate and sugar. Do not let the mixture get too hot. Remove it from the heat and stir in 4 egg yolks, rum, powdered coffee and pinch of cinnamon. Leave as is and cook over low heat, stirring frequently, until it regains its original consistency.

Remove the chocolate base from the heat and gently fold in the 4 stiffly beaten egg whites. There may be white streaks here and there, but it doesn't matter as long as you've been careful not to break down those bubbles beaten in the egg whites. Pour the mixture into a buttered 1-pint soufflé dish and bake the soufflé in moderate oven (350°) for about 25 minutes. Properly baked, the soufflé should be slightly undercooked. Sprinkle the top with confectioners' sugar and serve immediately.

Serves 4.

Barley Soufflé

This dessert has a mind of its own. It was born full grown at a lovely dinner party given by Mr. and Mrs. David May. They thought it was accidental. I know you'll agree with me after hearing my story that it was no accident. Dee and David gave the menu for one of their lovely little dinner parties to their Chinese Chef, a fine cook who at that time did not speak or understand English too well. Accompanying the meat, along with a couple of other vegetables, was to be a Barley Soufflé or casserole. The entrée came and went and there was no Barley Soufflé, but for dessert the chef came in proudly bearing an incredibly beautiful soufflé complete with a choice of caramel or fudge sauce. It was the Barley Soufflé and it is now one of their most-in-demand desserts.

I asked Mr. Cheung Wan Yip for the recipe. He gave it to me and I handed it to the boss—Pauline. One evening, with the meat course, Pauline proudly marched in bearing that beautiful Barley Soufflé—as a vegetable.

Try this one—as a dessert, if it will let you—with a hot Caramel Sauce (page159) or a Fudge Sauce (page165). It's as delicious as it is capricious.

❧

8 egg whites	4-ounce package of cream cheese
½ cup barley	Juice of ½ lemon
4 egg yolks	¾ cup sugar

Grease a 7-inch soufflé dish with butter and sprinkle granulated sugar in soufflé dish, tipping so that it covers all sides. Make a 2½-inch collar of wax paper to circle soufflé dish. Butter wax paper and tie around soufflé dish with a piece of string. Then cook barley according to directions on package. Drain if any liquid is remaining.

Add ½ cup of sugar and lemon juice. Mix well. Beat 2 egg yolks one at a time into barley and mix well. In a separate bowl, mix the cream cheese with the two remaining beaten egg yolks. Stir into barley mixture. Beat egg whites until stiff but not dry. Add remaining ¼ cup of sugar. Stir ½ cup of egg whites into the barley mixture. Stir well. Then fold remaining egg whites into the barley mixture very carefully, using a rubber spatula to blend the heavier barley mixture with lighter egg whites. Don't overfold or you'll lose all the air you have beaten into the egg whites. There'll be some streaks of egg white as you carefully (use a spatula) pour the barley mixture into soufflé dish.

Bake in a preheated 400° oven for 20 minutes. Reduce oven temperature to 375° and bake for an additional 15 minutes.

Serves 4 to 6.

Cakes and Cookies

❀

Mother's Pecan Rum Cakes

These are something special! In the good old days in Winchester, Tennessee, when all mothers were plump and forced everybody to eat a little more, Mother used to serve, at her ladies' bridge club luncheons, her special chicken or crab meat salad with piping hot homemade rolls—and then these—probably with homemade ice cream. Just a little something to keep body and soul together until they'd go home to cook dinner.

❀

4 egg whites (let egg whites warm to room temperature)
2¼ cups sifted cake flour
1½ cups sugar
3½ teaspoons baking powder
½ cup softened butter, margarine or shortening

1 teaspoon salt
¾ cup milk
1½ teaspoons vanilla
½ teaspoon rum extract
¼ cup rum
Pecans, finely chopped

Preheat oven to 350°.

Sift flour, sugar, salt and baking powder into large bowl of mixer. Add shortening or butter, milk and vanilla. Beat on slow speed until blended. Then beat at medium speed for 2 minutes, occasionally scraping sides of bowl with rubber scraper. Add unbeaten egg whites, rum extract and rum. Beat 2 minutes longer at medium speed. Pour batter into one long 13 x 9 x 2½-inch pan (or two 8-inch pans) that has been greased and floured and lined with wax paper. Bake for 35 to 40 minutes or until surface springs back when gently pressed with finger tips. Let cake cool and prepare icing (see next page).

Icing

½ cup butter (1 stick)
¾ pound confectioners' sugar, sifted
    (scant 3 cups)

4 tablespoons milk
1½ teaspoons vanilla
Salt

Cream butter and sugar with hand beater until fluffy. Add salt and stir in milk. Keep beating until very fluffy. Add vanilla.

Cut cake into 1½-inch squares. Pour a generous teaspoon of rum on each cake square. Spread icing on all sides and roll in chopped fresh pecans. The icing part is pretty messy, but it all comes out beautifully as you roll it around in the chopped nuts. I use a chopping bowl for this. You can substitute moist coconut for nuts and you have Snow Rum Balls instead of Pecan Rum Cakes. Or, if you leave out the rum, you have plain Snow Balls, which are great too. Make them 2½-inches square and you have a dessert dish instead of an accompaniment.

Makes about 40 little cakes.

The Losers' Coffee Cake

I lived in Palm Springs for a year. During that time I improved my tennis, golf and gin rummy games—there was hardly any other way for any of them to go. Before I became the card shark I am today (sic), I played with a group of ladies who used to throw parties for me when they heard I was available. Throw parties? They'd send taxicabs, limousines, airplanes—anything for their pigeon. It was fun, though, and one of the happier incidental benefits among the losings was this coffee cake recipe one of the ladies served from time to time.

❧

Dough

¼ pound margarine or butter
1 cup sugar
2 eggs
1 pint sour cream
2 cups cake flour

1 teaspoon soda
1 teaspoon baking powder
Dash of salt
1 teaspoon vanilla

Cream the butter or margarine with sugar. Add the eggs and sour cream. Sift together the cake flour, soda, baking powder and salt, and add to the creamy mixture. Then mix in the vanilla.

Filling

⅓ cup sugar	¾ cup nuts
1 teaspoon cinnamon	¾ cup chocolate bits

Mix ingredients together. In greased angel food cake pan, put a layer of dough, layer of filling, layer of dough, layer of filling. Bake in 350° oven for 40 minutes.

Serves 8.

Cinnamon Pound Cake

Very Good + Easy

One season when we lived in Palm Springs, Jody's close friend was a boy named Kenny Minasian. Jody loved to go to Kenny's house after school. I thought we ought to return the favor and have Kenny visit us. They tried it a couple of times—but almost always ended up at Kenny's. His mother's Cinnamon Pound Cake was the reason why. It's so good I wanted to go over and play too!

❀

¼ cup sugar	½ cup high grade margarine
⅛ cup cinnamon	(or butter)
3 cups sifted flour	1⅔ cups sugar
3 teaspoons baking powder	1 teaspoon vanilla
½ teaspoon salt	4 eggs
½ cup butter	1 cup milk

Preheat the oven to 350° and grease a 10-inch tube pan. Mix together the ¼ cup sugar and cinnamon and set aside. Sift together the flour, baking powder and salt and set aside also. Cream together the butter, margarine (or butter) and 1⅔ cups sugar until real fluffy. Add vanilla and eggs and beat until fluffy. Alternately add the milk and flour to the mixture. Put a layer of dough in the cake pan (half of batter). Sprinkle half of the cinnamon mixture over the batter, cover with remaining batter and top with remaining cinnamon mixture. Bake for 1 hour. Cake must be thoroughly cooled before cutting.

Serves 10 to 12.

Coconut Pound Cake

6 eggs
1 cup shortening
½ cup butter or margarine
3 cups sugar
½ teaspoon almond extract
½ teaspoon coconut extract

1 teaspoon baking powder
3 cups sifted cake flour
1 cup milk
2 cups grated fresh coconut or
    canned flaked coconut

Separate eggs, placing whites in a large bowl, yolks in another large bowl. Let egg whites warm to room temperature—about 1 hour. Preheat oven to 300° and grease a 10-inch tube pan.

With electric mixer at high speed, beat egg yolks with shortening and margarine until well blended. Gradually add sugar, beating until light and fluffy. Add extracts; beat until blended. At low speed, beat in flour (in fourths) alternately with milk (in thirds), beginning and ending with flour. Add coconut; beat until well blended. Beat egg whites just until stiff peaks form. With wire whisk or rubber scraper, gently fold whites into batter until well combined. Turn into prepared pan. Bake 2 hours or until cake tester inserted near center comes out clean. Cool in pan on wire rack 15 minutes. Remove cake from pan; cool thoroughly on wire rack. Before serving, dust top lightly with confectioners' sugar.

Serves 12 to 16.

Pauline's German Sweet Chocolate Cake

4 ounces Baker's German sweet
    chocolate
½ cup boiling water
1 cup butter
2 cups sugar
4 egg yolks, unbeaten

1 teaspoon vanilla
2½ cups sifted cake flour
½ teaspoon salt
1 teaspoon baking soda
1 cup buttermilk
4 egg whites, stiffly beaten

Melt chocolate in boiling water. Cool. Cream butter and sugar until fluffy. Add egg yolks, one at a time, and beat well after each addition. Add melted chocolate and vanilla. Mix well.

Sift together flour, salt and soda. Add alternately with buttermilk to chocolate mixture, beating after each addition until smooth. Fold in beaten egg whites. Pour into three 8- or 9-inch layer pans, lined on bottoms with paper. Bake at 350° for 30 to 40 minutes. Cool. Frost as indicated below.

Coconut-Pecan Frosting and Filling

1 cup evaporated milk
1 cup sugar
3 egg yolks
½ cup butter

1 teaspoon vanilla
2 cups coconut, flaked
1½ cups pecans, chopped

Combine the evaporated milk, sugar, egg yolks, butter and vanilla. Cook and stir over medium heat until thickened—about 12 minutes. Add the coconut and pecans. Beat until thick enough to spread. Use frosting as filling between layers and frost tops and sides.

Serves 12 to 16.

Fanny Brice's Super Chocolate Cake

4 squares bitter chocolate
¼ pound butter
1 cup hot water
2 cups flour
2 cups sugar

Pinch of salt
½ cup buttermilk
1¼ teaspoon soda
2 eggs, beaten
1 teaspoon vanilla

Melt the chocolate in a double boiler in the cup of hot water. Bring to a boil. Mix the chocolate and melted butter. Sift the flour, sugar and salt. Pour the chocolate and butter all at once into the dry ingredients and blend well. Add buttermilk and soda and mix well. Then add the eggs and vanilla. Bake in 350° oven for almost 30 minutes. While the cake is in the oven, prepare the frosting (see next page). Frost while warm.

Frosting

4 squares bitter chocolate
7 tablespoons milk
3 cups sifted powdered sugar

1 tablespoon vanilla
3 tablespoons melted butter
Pinch of salt

Melt the bitter chocolate in a double boiler. Mix the milk and powdered sugar and add the chocolate and vanilla. Then add the melted butter and salt.

Serves 8 to 10.

Chocolate Date Cake with Whipped Cream Topping

4 egg yolks
1 cup sugar
1 tablespoon orange juice
2 tablespoons chocolate, grated or powdered

3 tablespoons flour
1 teaspoon baking powder
1 cup dates, chopped
1 cup walnuts, chopped
4 egg whites

Cream egg yolks with sugar until light, then stir in orange juice. Sift flour with grated or powdered chocolate and baking powder. Sift second time into egg yolk mixture. Dredge chopped dates and walnuts with flour and fold into batter. Beat egg whites until stiff and fold gently into the mixture. Bake in a 325° oven for 45 to 50 minutes.

Whipped Cream Topping

1 cup heavy cream
¼ cup sugar

1 tablespoon vanilla
Dates, pitted for garnish

Whip heavy cream until stiff. Sweeten with sugar and flavor with vanilla. Ice top and sides of cake with the cream and decorate top with dates.

Serves 6 to 8.

Pecan Nut Balls

½ pound butter
4 tablespoons granulated sugar
2 teaspoons vanilla

2 cups cake flour
2 cups pecans, chopped
Powdered sugar

Cream butter, sugar and vanilla. Sift and add flour. Add nuts. Cream well until dough cleans bowl, adding a little more flour if necessary. Form dough into small balls about ¾ inch in diameter or roll into finger shapes. Place on ungreased cookie sheet ¼ inch apart. Bake in preheated 300° oven (moderate) until light straw color (about 25 to 30 minutes depending on oven). Immediately roll hot cookies in powdered sugar and again when cold. These will keep well in an airtight tin.
Makes about 60 cookies.

Cheesecake Cookies

⅓ cup butter, melted
⅓ cup brown sugar, packed
1 cup flour
½ cup walnuts, chopped
1 8-ounce package cream cheese

¼ cup sugar
1 egg
1 tablespoon lemon juice
2 tablespoons cream or milk
1 teaspoon vanilla

Mix brown sugar, chopped nuts and flour together in a large bowl. Stir in the melted butter and mix with your hands until light and crumbly. Remove 1 cup of the mixture to be used later as a topping. Place remainder in an 8-inch square pan and press firmly. Bake at 350° for about 12 or 15 minutes.

Beat cream cheese until smooth with the ¼ cup of sugar. Beat in the egg, lemon juice, milk and vanilla. Pour this onto the baked crust.

Top with the reserved crumbs. Return to a 350° oven and bake for about 25 minutes. Cool thoroughly, then cut into two-inch squares.

These can be baked the day before. Cover with plastic wrap and keep refrigerated.

Makes about 16 cookies.

Quality Coconut Cookies in Quantity

3½ cups moist coconut, shredded
    and chopped
2 cups flour, sifted
½ teaspoon baking soda
1 cup butter or margarine
½ teaspoon vanilla extract

1 cup sugar
1 egg, well beaten
1½ cups pecan halves
1 egg yolk
1 tablespoon cream
½ cup white corn syrup

Sift together the flour and baking soda and set aside. Cream butter or margarine until it is softened and gradually add vanilla, creaming until fluffy after each addition. Add sugar in thirds, beating thoroughly after each addition. Blend egg and 2 cups of coconut in bowl. Mix thoroughly. Stir in dry ingredients. Knead lightly with finger tips 5 to 10 times or until mixture holds together.

Spread remaining coconut onto waxed paper. Form dough into 6 rolls about 1 inch in diameter. Roll in coconut. Wrap in waxed paper and place in refrigerator for at least 3 hours.

Meanwhile, lightly grease cookie sheets. Remove rolls from refrigerator and, with a sharp knife, slice crosswise in half-inch slices. Place on cookie sheets ¾ inch apart. Mix egg yolk and cream together and brush cookie tops with mixture. Press a pecan half on top of each cookie. Bake at 325° about 20 minutes or until very lightly browned. Remove to cooling rack. Heat the syrup until warm. Glaze pecan and cookie by brushing with the warm corn syrup.

Yields a larger number of cookies than you should eat at one sitting—over 100, anyway.

Toffee Coffee Ice Cream Cake

1 angel food cake (a store-bought one
   will do if you're in a hurry)
Coffee ice cream
½ pint whipping cream

Sugar
1 teaspoon instant coffee
English toffee candy

Slice angel food cake crosswise twice, making 3 layers. Spread generous layer of coffee ice cream about an inch or more thick on the two lower layers. Replace top. Make icing as follows:

Icing

Whip the cream; add sugar and taste. Use a spoonful of instant coffee to give it mocha color and flavor. Cover the entire cake with it. Break English toffee into small bits and sprinkle generously over the entire cake. Chill in refrigerator until ready to serve.

Delay assembling this as long as you can. The refrigerator is fine for the icing but not so good for the coffee ice cream—the freezer is fine for the coffee ice cream but plays funny tricks with the whipped cream toffee icing.

Serves 6 to 8.

Fruit Cake

We used to do what I subsequently learned is a kind of a square thing. We lived in this little house on a lot of land in Encino, California. Until we remodeled it, I had only a small kitchen. On the "lot of land" we had practically everything the San Fernando Valley could produce in the way of fruit—plums, apricots, peaches, grapefruit, wild orange and domestic orange, limes, lemons, grapes, kumquats—you name it—we had it. We would harvest these things and I would make my conserves, jellies and jams and then I'd bake my fruit cakes. There was no way to compete with some of the expensive store-bought gifts our group kept passing around to each other, so George would make a simple, beautiful wooden tray and on it I would place the fruit cake and whatever jams, jellies and conserves turned out well and give them to special friends at Christmastime.

This is the recipe I used for fruit cake. I don't exactly know where I got it—probably a combination of many—but the true test of its success is how badly you bruised your toes if the cake happened to fall on them. Since they are too hard to make, I didn't drop too many so I have to assume they were good. It takes a lot of time and effort to make it and assemble it—and to season it properly—but don't forget you can start in October to make these for Christmas.

Open it up every week and sprinkle a little brandy on the underside of it—then wrap it up tightly. Since Christmas is for children—if you've been really conscientious about the brandy applications—I would suggest you wait until New Year's Eve. You'll never believe how smashing this can be while the guys are watching the Rose Bowl Game on New Year's Day. If they'd rather have beans and beer, slice it very thin (remember—nobody can handle a big chunk of fruit cake) and serve it to the girls. It will keep six months to a year if you seal it right.

2 cups brown sugar
2 cups butter
4 cups flour
12 eggs, beaten separately
2 teaspoons cinnamon
¼ pound candied orange rind
¼ pound candied lemon rind
1 pound figs
½ pound (generous) unbroken pecans
2 pounds raisins, seedless and white

1 pound dates, pitted
1 pound candied pineapple rings
1 teaspoon soda
1 teaspoon grated nutmeg
1 teaspoon cloves
¼ pound citron
½ cup molasses
½ pound blanched almonds
1 pound candied cherries
½ cup brandy
½ pound English walnuts

Remove stem end from figs, cut in half lengthwise; pit and cut dates in half, mix with 1 cup flour; cut each ring pineapple into two slices and then in half crosswise. Mix rest of flour with soda and spices. Cream butter, add sugar, then well-beaten egg yolks and stir well. Add flour mixture alternately with liquids. Add dates, figs and raisins. Gently fold in beaten egg whites. Line with waxed paper, leaving tabs up on sides to make removal from pans easy. Put in layer of batter, then row of pineapple down center, fill sides and spaces with citron, orange, lemon, nuts and cherries, another layer of batter, etc. Top with batter and decorate top with almonds or pecans, and cherries.

Have pans no more than ⅔ full. Set pans in 300° oven in pan filled with one inch of hot water. Bake half an hour. Cover with paper, bake 2 hours longer. Remove from water and bake half an hour more in slow oven. Remove from pans immediately. Remove paper. When cool, wrap in fresh wax paper and aluminum foil for storage.

Makes 6 cakes in 7-inch round pans or 7½ x 4-inch loaf pans.